Ultimate Travel: Depoe Bay

and Surrounding Area

Every Beach Access, Odd Facts, Fun Finds

Word and Photos by Andre' GW Hagestedt

To find more on Depoe Bay (including lodging) see
www.beachconnection.net/depoebay

All content and photos (except for those credited to Seaside Aquarium) copyright Andre' GW Hagestedt

Table of Contents

HOW TO USE THIS BOOK..5
INTRODUCTION...6
DEPOE BAY QUICK ACCESS GUIDE..8
GENERAL DEPOE BAY, GLENEDEN BEACH DETAILED
GUIDE...19
   BEACH SAFETY..20
GENERAL FEATURES, ADVICE, SECRETS, FUN FINDS....22
   Seasons of Depoe Bay..22
   Depoe Bay Nightlife...23
Beachcombing In and Around Depoe Bay..24
Year-round Resident Whales of Depoe Bay......................................27
   Insiders Tips on Spotting Whales...30
   Bald Eagles of Depoe Bay..32
   Tidepools..33
   Do Not Feed the Birds or Wildlife...33
   Second Summer..35
   Early Spring of February..37
   Secret Spring...39
That Slippery, Dangerous Green Goo..42
Secret But Year-round Ghost Forests of Otter Rock........................44
   Ghost Forests of Moolack Beach...48
Unusual Sights – Rarities in General...49
DETAILED GUIDE TO DEPOE BAY..53
   Coming from the North: Lincoln City, Salishan, Kernville....53
   Salishan and Salishan Spit..54
Gleneden Beach...55
   History of Gleneden Beach..56
Hidden Access of Gleneden Beach...58
Gleneden Beach State Recreation Area...59
Lincoln Beach..61
   Wallace St. Access..62
Fishing Rock State Recreation Site...63
Fogarty Beach State Recreation Area..68
   Exploring That Secret Beach...71
   Odd Facts: Mysterious Shapes at Fogarty Beach..........................72

Boiler Bay Gravel Viewpoint..75
    Secret Part of Oregon Coast Trail...77
Boiler Bay State Scenic Viewpoint..80
Exploding Ship Near Depoe Bay: How Boiler Bay Got Its Name
....82
Northern Depoe Bay..86
Secret Access: North Point...87
Downtown Depoe Bay..91
History of Depoe Bay..92
    Whale Watch Center, Depoe Bay..94
Depoe Bay Landmark: Spouting Horn...95
Poking Around Pillow Basalt of the Oregon Coast.....................97
Depoe Bay Bridge and History...101
Depoe Bay History: Tsunami Damage of 2011 and 1964..........103
    Depoe Bay – the Bay and Shell Ave....................................106
    World's Smallest Navigable Harbor.....................................107
    Depoe Bay Whale and Shark Museum.................................107
    Depoe Bay Visitors Center / Chamber.................................107
Secret Spots: Viewpoints Behind Downtown............................108
Depoe Bay's Teeny, Tiny Secret Park...109
Hidden Access: South Point...112
Whale Cove and Little Whale Cove Island Reserve..................113
Rocky Creek State Scenic Viewpoint..114
Roaring Ledges of Rodea Point..119
    Hiking the Oregon Coast Trail South of Depoe Bay............121
Otter Crest Loop..122
    Ben Jones Bridge – Rocky Creek and Ben Jones Bridge
    Viewpoint..124
    Otter Crest Loop Begins – Wacky History..........................126
    Secret Spot: Cliffs Below Otter Crest Loop Road................128
    Viewpoints Along the One-Way...130
Cape Foulweather...131
Weird Science: Cape Foulweather Geology..............................133
Otter Rock – Town and Rock Structure.....................................135
    History: Naming Otter Rock, Devil's Punchbowl.................135
    History: Ben Jones, "Father of Highway 101".....................139
Landmark: Devil's Punchbowl, Devil's Punchbowl State Scenic

Natural Area..140
    Inside Devil's Punchbowl..142
    Marine Gardens Near Depoe Bay...143
    Odd History: Little Men of the Punchbowl..........................146
Odd History: Elephant Rock at the Punchbowl, Legends..........147
Origin of Devil's Punchbowl: Trippy Geology........................150
Odd Find: Secret Ghost Forest Stump......................................152
Local History: Pathfinders and Primitive Roads......................152
    ABOUT ANDRE' GW HAGESTEDT......................................154

HOW TO USE THIS BOOK

This guide to Depoe Bay and the surrounding area is set up in three main parts: the Quick Guide of each beach access and attraction, general beach facts and travel advice for the area – and then a much more detailed guide to all those beaches and attractions with the full meal deal of gobs and oodles of unique information, history, oddities, secrets and more.

The detailed section you may find cumbersome if you're actually on the coast or in the middle of trip planning, and you don't want to wade through all the deeper stuff. So the beach Quick Guide will allow you to skim quickly as you're on the road, giving you a brief look at where you're going. But the true fun is in all the details, oddities, secrets and history – which you can bounce down to at any time.

Milepost markers are used whenever possible, as in "MP 22." These are the little green signs by the sides of the highway with such numbers, and they start at 0 in Astoria and get bigger as you head south. These guides also work their way from north to south. However, since most attractions and beaches are far off 101, this book doesn't utilize a lot of these markers.

To find lodging in Depoe Bay, see www.beachconnection.net/depoebay. This also contains even more details and updated articles about Depoe Bay, the virtual tour that includes maps, as well as food / dining listings.

For more images of these subjects, link suggestions are provided – or simply to go BeachConnection.net and do a search on that subject. Full color photos will be in great abundance there.

INTRODUCTION

Rocky blobs and globs as far as the eye can see, smacked around by gargantuan waves – all surrounded by thick, forested greens. What's not to love about the Depoe Bay area? It's got rugged beauty, crazy drama and an astounding number of hidden spots.

This section of the coast is sadly a bit overlooked – because it's not exactly the beach. Yet it probably has more to offer in terms of sheer surprises and eye-popping moments than most areas of the entire shoreline. There's certainly more jam-packed into the four miles on either side of Depoe Bay than you'll know what to do with. Between the softer sands of Gleneden Beach down to the soaring vistas of Otter Rock – probably about six miles – you couldn't explore it all in one day. There's that much.

Some of its most impressive wonders are a bit tucked away. The headland of Fishing Rock is one such stunner, which sits hidden behind trees and a suburban street. It's not a hidden spot, being a state park. No one knows about it because it's hard to see. The same with Rodea Point, where some of the most spectacular wave action takes place on a regular basis, as well as with the rest of the Otter Crest Loop drive – another beauty hiding in plain sight.

Again, my whole intent behind this Ultimate Oregon Coast Travel series is to bring entire new levels of enjoyment possibilities to the surface. You're going to dig your trip even more if you know what you're looking at. Few sections of the coastline typify this more, largely because there's so much hidden away. In this case, you'll enjoy this area more if you know where to find the cool stuff. After that, if some sights get explained, you've got yet another level of awe to let sweep over you.

Local history in these parts has some unique aspects, especially the geology of it. Some startling stuff there. There's some delightfully odd surprises, like the "little flying men" of Devil's Punchbowl, or the area's connection to the great man who really kickstarted Highway 101. Plus, the crazy adventures of the shipwreck that gave Boiler Bay its name: it feels like an action movie that hasn't been made yet.

Then for a real jolt of fun, what whales around here are capable of doing will provide some serious delights. I was amazed when running across these tidbits.

The amusing thing about this book series is I really (well, sort of) screwed up on the last one, about Lincoln City. While that one includes Gleneden Beach in the title, there's actually more on Gleneden Beach in this book. As I was digging further into Gleneden Beach, its history and through my own endless archive of photos, I discovered more on the tiny town. I simply had to include all the new finds here. So, yes, you'll actually have to get this one and the Lincoln City book to get the full story on Gleneden Beach.

So much of this book was compiled over some 25 years of visiting the area over and over, and always falling in love with it a little more. Still, a good deal of material was uncovered at the last minute, and this Depoe Bay installment has been a headrush of discoveries.

Here's hoping you get the same out of this that I did.

- Andre' GW Hagestedt

Publisher, Oregon Coast Beach Connection

DEPOE BAY QUICK ACCESS GUIDE

Salishan and Salishan Spit

A famous hiking spot and an upscale business complex are the two main features here. Oh, and there is a golf course. If you're a hotel guest or a resident of the gated community, you have access to the beach from here. Otherwise, the northernmost beach access that allows you to hike the spit is down in Gleneden Beach quite a ways.

Gleneden Beach

This tiny community south of Lincoln City has a smattering of restaurants, a community hall and sporadic vacation rentals, but no real hotel.

The real attraction is simply the beach – and it's a curious set of beaches too. Also notable about these beaches is the proliferation of larger, coarser sand grains, and some tracts of blackish sands.

Hidden Access of Gleneden Beach

Off Gleneden Beach Loop, a couple of streets will lead you to beach entrances, including your best bet for accessing Salishan Spit because of the locked gate farther north.

Wander west down Sijota St. until you reach Neptune St. and a hidden access there. Miles and miles of fluffy sand await you. This is the northernmost access towards the Spit.

Gleneden Beach State Recreation Area

Near milepost 122, a ways after Lincoln City and the Salishan area, and just before you get to the Lincoln Beach area, sits this gem of a state park. Picnic tables, a small lawn area, and a picnic shelter for groups are also highlights on this grass-covered plot above the beach. There are restrooms aplenty as well.

Descend down a fairly short path, through a thick forested stretch, and you'll find the opening to this magnificent and rather unique beach.

Lincoln Beach

Lincoln Beach sits a mile south of Gleneden Beach and about two miles north of Depoe Bay. Like Gleneden Beach, this stretch is often full of coarser, larger grains of sand and steep tidelines. A couple of tiny, barely-marked beach accesses sit amid the neighborhoods.

Wallace St. Access

It's the final access of Lincoln Beach – just look for Wallace St. and follow it to its end. This is an interesting one, with rather intricate cliffs, some giant blob rocks to break up the scenery, and one really weather-beaten tree that's somewhat remarkable. This is a great storm watching spot – from the road, that is.

Fishing Rock State Recreation Site

As the Lincoln Beach area ends, a tad north of milepost 125, it lies tucked away, just out of sight. What stands out here are the wild colors of the cliffs, the craggy, rocky basalt edges that form mesmerizingly cool structures to climb around on, and a variety of large-scale and miniature viewpoints that are always cause for dropping of the jaw.

Fogarty Beach State Recreation Area

A spot full of wonders both subtle and standing in plain view. You start out trudging through a thick forest canopy that hides a few nooks and crannies of its own. Features include lots of weird rock structures (see the full listing).

Boiler Bay Gravel Viewpoint

A small gravel parking lot at the top leads to a rather steep and boulder-laden trail snaking its way down to the bay. At higher tides there's very little beach here, and even at lower tides it's mostly a labyrinth of rocky slabs and stones, sometimes covered with that nasty, green algae that'll make you slip and fall on your head in a split second. However, the fun of Boiler Bay lies in its awesome tidepools, clandestine caves and meandering paths over and around its mostly rocky landscape. If the tide is low enough, you get better views of the old boiler.

Secret Part of Oregon Coast Trail

As you park at the gravel pullout of Boiler Bay, you may notice a nondescript little sign that says Oregon Coast Trail. Continue down this path for some remarkable secrets. It's part of the Boiler Bay to Fogarty Creek portion of the Oregon Coast Trail, running just over a mile before it meets up with Fogarty Beach at the northern end.

Boiler Bay State Scenic Viewpoint

Some of this sprawling, grass-covered treasure contains a few nooks and crannies that are a bit hard to find. It is powerfully scenic, with equally powerful waves rumbling past.

Restrooms, picnic tables and plenty of stunning views abound here. A nice, long lawn-like area provides a slightly pastoral experience as you take in the ocean air, and maybe walk your dog a tad. Lined with a rustic log fence, you can lean over just a bit and take in a tiny splash of ocean mist on your face from these fairly rambunctious waves.

Northern Depoe Bay

Traffic alert: police can patrol this town with more frequency than other coastal towns, often in unmarked vehicles. Watch your speed here.

You enter a business district with plenty of condos, then about a half a mile into town you'll encounter a sidewalk with a barrier, and there's a bit of a secret viewpoint here. You can look out over the cove that spreads between the condos and the mini-headland called North Point.

Secret Access: North Point

Look for Vista Ave. or Sunset Ave., then follow it to its end.

That arm of black rock that stretches out from the northern edge of Depoe Bay? (If you're looking from the seawall). That's it – and it is called North Point. It is one spectacular stretch of clandestine cliffs that are hiding in plain sight.

You'll find a lot lurking in this slice of coastline that is perhaps a mere one eighth of a mile long, which is tucked away behind a handful of neighborhood streets at the northern end of Depoe Bay. You can't really see it from anywhere – except that part of it that juts out into view from downtown Depoe. Even the actual accesses are difficult to spot as you drive by them.

Downtown Depoe Bay

Part tourist trap and part natural spectacle, and it's an irresistible and yet tranquil stop while zipping through the central Oregon coast. Depoe Bay's downtown area consists of about two or three blocks worth of businesses - an area crammed with curio shops, restaurants of all sizes and cost ranges, along with a stunning view of the ocean.

Whale Watch Center, Depoe Bay

Headquarters to the Whale Watch Spoken Here program that operates the twice-yearly Whale Watch Weeks, here you can hang out and learn a lot about whales as well as see them. Staff are always present to help you see whales in the Depoe Bay area. They can create quite the eye-popping display as they dive, shoot out their blowholes, spyhop and breach. Located at the southern end of the Depoe Bay Bridge, right next to the bay, on Hwy 101, Depoe Bay, Oregon. (541) 765-3407 and (541) 765-3304. www.whalespoken.org.

Depoe Bay Landmark: Spouting Horn

A large crevice in the basalt rocks of Depoe Bay near the sea wall is known to compress sea water and then fire it into the air in a spectacular, energetic display. This oceanic geyser can reach 40 feet or more, creating an enormous plume. This requires higher tides or larger wave height – or both.

Depoe Bay – the Bay and Shell Ave.

On the southern side of the bridge you'll find the vehicle entrance to the bay. Down here, there's plenty o' parking for big rigs with boats in tow, fish-cleaning facilities, and an all around sense of calm and serenity as the waves gently plop and splash against the docks and pavement.

At night, this is especially lovely, with the lights dancing on the water and the stars gleaming overhead. That is, if the stars are showing, of course.

World's Smallest Navigable Harbor

Depoe Bay boasts the claim of "world's smallest navigable harbor," but in fact there is no official designation of any such thing. No one's keeping real records on this. But in any case, it is charming and it certainly is tiny, and there's surprisingly a lot to see.

Besides the thrill of watching vessels wandering in and out, simply checking out this body of water from the bridge viewpoints just below the bridge is a kick.

Depoe Bay Whale and Shark Museum

A variety of deep insights into the whales, sharks and other sea critters of the coastline. Entrance fee. 234 US-101, Depoe Bay, Oregon. (541) 912-6734

Depoe Bay Visitors Center / Chamber

Gobs of information about the Depoe Bay area, including lots of regional brochures you can't get online. 223 US-101, Depoe Bay, Oregon. Www.depoebaychamber.org. (877) 485-8348.

Secret Spots: Viewpoints Behind Downtown

On the very southern edge of the bridge sit two stellar yet unknown features of Depoe Bay. Two secret diminutive viewpoints hide behind the building containing the visitor center.

The first viewpoint is part of the lawn area found between the first two buildings on that southern edge of the bridge. You can walk down the grassy slope a bit and take in a closer look at the vessels wandering the channel, or simply get a different and really interesting new angle on the bridge and the bay. It's not a bad patch of ground to watch for whales.

The second sits sort of behind the Depoe Bay Chamber building. 50 feet from 101, a strictly one-way road then turns into Coast Drive. At that intersection, another small viewpoint sits: simply a bench on a slight and paved outcropping.

Depoe Bay's Teeny, Tiny Secret Park

Tucked away behind a bundle of bushes and trees, along a cliffside road that's much less traveled, the tiny space is full of eye-popping views. Yet it's unknown to even many locals. The miniature park is hidden behind an even tinier entrance, which sits along Coast Drive, almost caddy corner from the back of the fire station (but about a block and a half down). Marked only by that small sign – which looks more like some whimsical lawn decoration at first glance – your only real clue is that small railing and three steps. Features: you're hidden behind a lot of brush with a bench and really lovely views to keep you company.

Hidden Access: South Point

At the extreme southern tip of town you have another deliriously engaging hidden spot. Look for South Point St., and you'll find a set of cliffs where few others are and where all sorts of wondrous things happen that don't occur anywhere else nearby.

Rocky Creek State Scenic Viewpoint

A sliver south of Depoe Bay. Rocky Creek State Scenic Viewpoint is essentially a set of cliffs that zig-zag along this part of the central coast between Newport and Depoe Bay, with basalt bluffs that cause the waves to batter on a consistent basis. Lofty vantage points grace practically every inch of it, allowing intense viewing of every splashy moment. They're high enough that it's easy to gaze over the top of the wild breakers and take in the more distant and calm sea surface beyond them.

There are restroom facilities here that make it a nice stop along your travels, but there are also a huge array of tremendous views to be had as the cliffs meander back and forth between viewing north, directly west and then looking to the south. A lengthy, sturdy fence along the sides of the cliffs keep you, your kids and pets from falling off the edges in most spots.

Roaring Ledges of Rodea Point

Almost immediately after the exit from Rocky Creek State Scenic Viewpoint you'll bump into Rodea Point, one of the area's great pleasures. This is yet another remarkable chunk of rocky shoreline where things explode more often than not.

Not well marked, Rodea Point is basically an informal viewpoint where a gravel pullout allows the traveler more means of watching massive waves do their pyrotechnics. In a lot of ways, it is a hidden spot. Or at least it's underutilized and overlooked.

Hiking the Oregon Coast Trail South of Depoe Bay

The trail runs along the highway and then down the sidewalks of Depoe Bay. At its southern end, hiking means walking the dangerous highway again a couple of miles until you reach Otter Crest Loop Road. There, a bike lane allows you a little more safety than the raging highway: at least cars are forced to move slowly here.

Then, you reach Cape Foulweather. From there, it's about a mile on the small roadway (now it's a two-lane stretch rather than one-way), until you reach Otter Rock and the Devil's Punchbowl. From there, descend the long stairway to Otter Rock's northern face, and you've got about four miles of beach to walk until 62nd St. at Newport.

Otter Crest Loop

This lulling but lively stretch of roadway is one of the more stunning along the Oregon coast, and yet it's fairly forgotten. Most of this road is one-way heading towards the south. The northern edge of Otter Crest Loop provides a nice assemblage of secretive wonders hiding in plain sight – along a tiny route which in itself is quite clandestine.

After a mile or so, you end up at the parking lot of Cape Foulweather and its astounding vistas.

Ben Jones Bridge – Rocky Creek and Ben Jones Bridge Viewpoint

A mere 100 feet after Rodea Point you'll bump into the Rocky Creek Bridge – also known as the Ben Jones Bridge. It was built in 1927 and stands at MP 130.03. There's a mini-turnout here to watch the surf go bonkers – and it does. There are no facilities here, but there's a rounded stone wall that boasts plenty of atmosphere and parking for a handful of cars. It's tiny but it's wondrous.

Secret Spot: Cliffs Below Otter Crest Loop Road

See the full listing.

Viewpoints Along the One-Way

Plunging cliffs disappear into raging surf. Dramatic ocean vistas pop out between the thick walls of soothing forest. Dazzling oceanic pyrotechnics are in abundance. Grassy greens cover the blackened basalt towers. Plus, you can see Cape Foulweather and the little gift shop atop it from new angles.

Every 200 to 300 feet there's some new, amazing sight to check out. Some pullouts are obvious; others look somewhat sketchy because they're so small you may be sticking your car out into traffic to some degree.

Cape Foulweather

Cape Foulweather stands about 500 feet above the sea, and is accessed by a somewhat winding tangle of roads that connect from a very twisting section of 101. Here, a small parking lot and viewpoint allow visitors panoramic vistas, including this magnificent nearly-aerial view of Otter Rock, its odd beaches and the famed Devil's Punchbowl below.

The other major feature is, of course, the gift shop, which has been there for decades. The old coastal stalwart still features those coin-operated telescope thing-a-ma-bobs.

Otter Rock – Town and Rock Structure

A ways down the road from Cape Foulweather – either via Otter Crest Loop or Highway 101 – the tiny burgh of Otter Rock sits tucked away atop this narrow promontory that includes the famed Devil's Punchbowl. It's an unincorporated community of a few hundred folks, if that, featuring a seafood joint, a rather famous winery operation and one or two seasonal shops, depending on the year or time of year.

Landmark: Devil's Punchbowl, Devil's Punchbowl State Scenic Natural Area

A giant sea cave that once caved in, its top is now open and the swirling oceanic display visible to all. It is a bit of a misnomer, however. The Devil's Punchbowl is not a fiery show a lot of the time, really.

This mini-headland and state park includes the marine gardens immediately to the north (the entrance is at the northern parking lot), and some stunning viewpoints to the south. From here you can see Newport, and in the distance the flashing of the Yaquina Head Lighthouse. There are some picnic tables and restroom facilities as well.

Marine Gardens Near Depoe Bay

While Devil's Punchbowl gets a lot of the attention, there's a stunning, rather unpopulated beach lying just below the cliffs that never ceases to cause wonder. During lower tide events is when the marine gardens appear. It's a tidepool hunter's paradise, with numerous critters existing here.

It's all accessed via a sloped walkway between the beach and the parking lot, and then the steps to the beach are sometimes non-existent or barely intact, as winter storms tend to ravage the boundaries of this beach.

Odd Find: Secret Ghost Forest Stump

A rather secret ghost forest resides near the bottom of the staircase below Otter Rock. Watch the tides: this isn't always accessible. The other one sits at the entrance to Beverly Beach.

GENERAL DEPOE BAY, GLENEDEN BEACH DETAILED GUIDE

BEACH SAFETY

Dangers in the Depoe Bay area are really in two parts: the small beaches with no escape, and the rocky slabs where you can fall in.

Winter storms and sneaker waves are the most prominent danger you have to worry about in the Gleneden Beach area, where most beaches are short enough to be deadly because there are cliff walls behind you that won't allow you to get away. A few people have died there thinking they were just taking a leisurely stroll on the beach while stormwatching. These beaches are small enough it doesn't take much of a tide to be a problem.

When you get down to the rocky stretches that typify Depoe Bay – from about Boiler Bay through to Devil's Punchbowl – there are plenty of fenced off sections in the first place, so you're okay as long as you don't climb beyond them. At the gravel parking lot of Boiler Bay, do NOT take that trail down if it's rainy or there's high tides. One couple disappeared without a trace there in the early 2000s.

Going beyond the seawall at downtown Depoe Bay will get you killed during storms: it happened in 2018. And some other cliff sections have no barriers – like several of the secret spots mentioned in this book. Don't touch these areas if the tides are unruly at all.

If you see a parking lot is closed off by city officials, heed that. People have been hurt by ignoring those warnings, usually from being knocked over by waves, and cars have been known to get swamped and ruined by salt water. One case in Garibaldi in the early 2000s saw a few cars actually floated for a time by a massive wave inundation, essentially considered totaled by the rush of salt water into components. The owners had ignored a closure sign.

See www.BeachConnection.net for the full spectrum of safety hazards, including swimming, tidepooling and more.

GENERAL FEATURES, ADVICE, SECRETS, FUN FINDS

Seasons of Depoe Bay

Not a lot happens in sleepy Depoe Bay when it comes to regular events, certainly yearly to-do's. There simply isn't a lot of room for community events, really. And the tiny town lacks the resources of larger cities like Lincoln City, Newport or even Rockaway Beach.

There are a handful of wacky summer offerings, like the Pirate Days, which is largely a commercial-oriented thing with some dressing up as pirates mixed in. Late summer features the salmon bake, where fish are cooked on sticks over fire pits in traditional native style. Fall tends to have a Halloween-themed event that involves ladies dressed as witches, which is a kick.

The big three you can count on are the tree-lighting ceremony in December, the somber Fleet Flowers (where they lay wreaths on the water to honor the fallen mariners) and the twice-yearly whale watch week. Every late December and Spring Break, volunteers join forces along dozens of high vantage points along the entire Oregon coast to help you spot whales. But the Depoe Bay area has the most of these Whale Spoken Here spots.

There is no Fourth of July celebration here because of impact to nests of endangered birds. Depoe Bay used to have a fantastic little Third of July show until the mid 2000s, when environmental impacts were discovered because of the pyrotechnics. Both Waldport and Depoe Bay held their fireworks displays on the third, while Pacific City often held theirs on the sixth – or thereabouts. So you wound up with the opportunity to enjoy three days of wild firework fun around Independence Day.

Stormwatching is the hot ticket item around here in winter: waves become gargantuan around those rocky shelves and do stunning things. Some can tower over you by 20, 30 feet at times. The spouting horn pulls off even more crazed stunts. It never gets old to watch. The sound of these impacting the rocks is insane as well: a massive, booming wallop sound at times.

Summer's highlights – and especially the Second Summer months of September and October – include soft, warm breezes and the paradoxically calm waves that simply lap at the rocks. It's just as stunning to see them do nothing as it is to be massive.

Spring holds more windy and wave-smacking wonders as well, with a mix of storms and sunny conditions. See the seasonal secrets section for full information.

Depoe Bay Nightlife

There's actually a vibrant little dive bar scene in Depoe Bay, although only one of them stays open later. Live music happens in a couple of the bar spots (one of them the lounge of a restaurant), and another is famous for its pizza and burgers but tends to be shut down by midnight or earlier. The Wing Wa (at least of this writing it's still called that) also has a smattering of live music sessions during weekends in the early evenings or afternoons, such as jazz or blues jams.

Karaoke is the big thing at the Wing Wa, however, and its kooky tiki lounge vibe is among the most delicious of most of the dive bars along the entire coast. If that's your thing – and God knows it isn't for everyone – Wing Wa is a must-see.

Beachcombing In and Around Depoe Bay

As most of Depoe Bay is actually rocky ledges, there's no sandy sections there for agates. These do exist sometimes around Gleneden Beach or just south of the area at the big beach of Otter Rock. However, rockhounding is more prolific just north in Lincoln City or south around Newport.

Also for the sandy stretches, the best oceanic goodies and oddities wash up in winter, fall and spring, just after storms. But summer features a few choice discoveries as well. Velella velella (those purple creatures that start to stink) tend to show up in early summer, sometimes scattered throughout the year. Also, pyrosomes have been making themselves at home – and a bit of a nuisance – in recent years, and no one knows why. More on those in coming sections. For even more information on this and more full color photos, see www.beachconnection.net.

For wilder oceanic fun, look for:

Whale burps are puzzling objects that look out of place on the beach: they resemble small stacks of hay, or sometimes they show up as balls of grassy stuff. In fact, they are bundles of beach grass or sea plants from the deep that have compacted so much that they're practically rock hard. This photo (above) was taken in Lincoln City.

Ocean burps are the largest, broadest class of stuff you'll discover. It really refers to a large potpourri of things – and it's different every time. There are a few items found in it more often than not, but mostly what makes this jumble of stuff connected is the fact it often shows up as a monumental, brownish pile of little bits.

Japanese Glass Floats are extremely rare, but it happens. Up north, Lincoln City, of course, is known for its Finders Keepers fun, which is now year-round.

Creatures on a Rope or Other Objects. When manmade objects spend a decent amount of time floating on or under the water, they usually acquire some kind of life form, which then remains on it if the chunk of flotsam winds up onshore. Sometimes, it's still alive.

Lancetfish. They look like a barracuda, and they are definitely somewhat rare (or certainly sporadic). It's actually called a Longnose Lancetfish (Alepisaurus ferox), and they live as far down as 6,000 feet below the surface. Reaching up to six feet in length, most that are found on the Oregon coast are three or four feet long. Even though they are common off these waters, they live so deep it's considered an unusual event when one washes up.

Pyrosome photo courtesy Seaside Aquarium's Tiffany Boothe

Pyrosomes. This is a bizarre creature that has suddenly started washing up along the Oregon coast in recent years. It's called a pyrosome, and the ones found here are less than a foot. They are actually massive colonies of cloned creatures all connected together – and slightly related to a kind of jellyfish called a salp.

Gobs of Bull Kelp. One of the more impressive but puzzling sights are giant piles of snake-like creatures of green or brown. These are bull kelp, and each individual can be several feet to twenty feet long. They exist in sizable kelp forests off the shoreline. You can see many of them from rocky shelf areas like those around Depoe Bay and Cape Foulweather, with their little brown heads bobbing in the ocean. For this reason they often get mistaken for seals.

Year-round Resident Whales of Depoe Bay

Thanks to a group of so-called "resident whales," Depoe Bay can bill itself as the "Whale Watching Capital of the World." There are gray whales who are regulars here, almost living in the area (but in fact the actual number varies and the group that lingers shifts and changes members).

Grays are attracted to the easy food pickings of the area, which in turn is thanks to all the bull kelp forests that grow up from these shallower depths and reefs.

Bull Kelp are a large, brown algae that grow in "forests" near the shore. These kelp are annuals, completing their life cycle in one season, and can grow up to 20 meters (60 feet) in one year. Mycid shrimp like to hide in these – and that's the shrimp that gray whales crave.

With such an abundance of bull kelp and thus mycid shrimp, that's what keeps the grays around this part of the central Oregon coast.

What exactly does it mean when they refer to "resident whales of Depoe Bay?"

Out of the 20,000 gray whales that live and migrate along the west coast, some 200 stop and hang out somewhere. According to Oregon Department of Fish and Wildlife's Marine Mammal Program Leader Sheanna Steingass, PhD, about 75 of those tend to loiter around the area between Newport and Depoe Bay on a regular basis.

That number of 75 – more actually, Steinglass said – is what comprises the so-called resident whales of Depoe Bay. At least that many have been documented returning again and again over the years. That doesn't mean there are 75 all the time loitering off these shores. Some dart out while others come back in; and then there are random whales that are migrating or simply moving through for whatever reason.

"For some individuals, there's that trade off between traveling that 10,000 miles up to Alaska every year or staying in Oregon where there's a fairly reliable food supply," Steinglass said.

That 75 or more has been accurately identified by people like Carrie Newell, Dr. Bruce Mate and other researchers off the coast. Steinglass said that individual whales from that group are easily recognized, and seen coming back year after year. It seems most are female, too. In fact, she said many mothers return with their calves and those babies learn the area, instilling in them the desire to return to Depoe Bay and the central coast. This gets passed on through generations of whales.

It's a trait held by many of the whales of the Pacific Northwest.

"Different whales select different areas to camp out during migration season," Steinglass said. "The ones in Newport and Depoe Bay tend to hang out in this area."

Gray whales are excellent for being able to identify the individuals, she said. They have discernible patterns and spots.

"Like killer whale rakes, or other scars that make them identifiable," Steinglass said. "One most visibly known – and I've seen her in Crescent City as well as the Oregon coast – is Scarback. She was apparently hit by an exploding harpoon in the mid '80s, probably in Russia. So she has this big gash on her back that's full of whale lice, and that makes it looks orange. So she's left alone by researchers and studies, but she's pretty friendly and she's come back year after year with calves."

In fact, when gray whales get friendly, some astounding sights result. If there's ever a reason to hit the whale tours of Depoe Bay or Newport, this is it. They are curious about us as well, and this makes for some unforgettable whale behaviors while on those cruises – sometimes. It's of course not guaranteed.

It's technically called "Friendly Behaviors." Steinglass pointed out some incredible experiences she had with mothers and babies off the Mexican coast, where they head to give birth every fall. It's a place that's free of sharks and killer whales, so they let their guard down.

"You can actually take boats, and the mothers will bring the babies up to the boats," she said. "Even to the point where they get under the babies and bring them out of the water so the baby can see people."

Those "friendly behaviors" lessen once they leave the safety of the lagoons, but gray whales have been known to do similar things on the Oregon coast.

A little more common in this area is the way they show their curiosity by spyhopping. That means briefly jumping out of the water to get a good look around.

"Several times while out tagging I've seen them spyhop behind you to get a better look at you, or hang around when there's no other reason to hang around," Steinglass said.

They have different personalities. Some are more standoffish, some are more curious. Steinglass notes one juvenile who got really cute by spyhopping behind her boat several times off Depoe Bay so it could check her out.

Then she drops a shocker: just how curious they can be and how close they can get to humans.

"It's amazing how close to shore they can get," she said. "I've seen videos of gray whales foraging in the surf zone, really close to people but they don't notice it. They can get into some pretty shallow water. I've seen videos of them within 20 to 30 feet of someone playing on the beach. You could see the whole whale."

Insiders Tips on Spotting Whales

While bouncing around Depoe Bay, it helps to watch the tour boats out there. If you see them lingering in one spot, keep an eye on the surrounding area. Often, they're there because of a whale showing itself. It's not long before you see that telltale whale spout or the vague, blackened shape of one moving in the water.

Other general tips from ODFW (for anywhere on the coast):

ODFW suggests finding a calm day and a high viewpoint, such as Neahkahnie Mountain near Manzanita, Cape Foulweather near Depoe Bay, Ecola State Park at Cannon Beach or the Cape Perpetua Visitors Center near Yachats – to name a few.

Low wave height is very important, as high waves act like trenches that hide the whales from view. Calm conditions – as well as not so stormy or foggy – make a big difference.

Also, you'll want to look out a few miles beyond shore.

"Learning good binocular technique will help spot the whales," ODFW said. "Gaze out onto the ocean, focusing on medium distances until you see a puff of white. Then raise your binoculars while continuing to look at the place you saw the puff. This technique takes some practice, but generally works better than swinging the binoculars around looking for something. Just keep your eyes focused on the whale and raise the binoculars to your eyes, looking through them, not into them."

Another great help is knowing how to spot them in the midst of the waves – what to look for.

"A gray whale's blow is up to 15 feet high, and each blow is visible for about five seconds," ODFW said. "When warm, moist air exhaled from the animals' lungs, meets the cool air at the ocean surface, it creates the bushy column called a blow, or spout. Anticipate that the whale will dive for three to six minutes, then surface for three to five blows in row, 30 to 50 seconds apart, before diving deep for three to six minutes again."

Much of Lincoln County is blessed with a good deal of whale action, though Lincoln City is at the northern edges of this activity and thus can see just a little less of it.

Also, the area gets a good dose of Orcas now and then.

There's almost always a rush of Orcas in the spring, usually running from about April into May, but recent years seem to have them show up a little sooner. These are a puzzling group of transient killer whales scientists know little about. They have a longer, more beak-like appearance. What is known is that they're here to chase the newborn gray whale calves that are migrating through with their mamas.

This creates a major spectacle sometimes as a killer whale is seen living up to its name by devouring a young gray whale in front of beachgoers, or maybe a seal or sea lion. It's gruesome but fascinating. That's a rare sight, but a little less rare – but not by much – is catching sight of the Orcas in hunting mode and chasing down something at high speed.

The Whale Watch Center in Depoe Bay notes that gray whales seem to know when the killer whales are in the area. Periodically, all the grays will abruptly disappear from the center's view, and after awhile – sure enough – some Orcas come plodding through the waters.

Bald Eagles of Depoe Bay

Bald eagles are spotted in all sorts of places along the Oregon coast, from the top of Oregon down to Brookings on the California border. They are certainly fairly frequent visitors here as well.

When to see them? Anytime of the year is equally good, according to nature expert Range Bayer, out of Newport. "We have a lot of resident adult bald eagles year-round along the Oregon coast," he said.

Bayer offered some tips for increasing your chances of spotting bald eagles. He said bays along the coast will help, like Alsea Bay at Waldport, Siletz Bay at Lincoln City, Netarts Bay at Oceanside, Florence's Siuslaw Bay, etc.

At the tideline is also a bit of a haunt for them, but given the close proximity to a lot of people that may be harder.

"Heading out on an outgoing tide is good," Bayer said. "You'll find them perched on pilings or logs. Looking up at the treelines of bays will help if you're trying to find adults."

Bayer said they're looking for fish and sometimes other birds.

Pauline Baker, with the North Coast Wildlife Rehabilitation Center near Astoria, said they are most active in the mornings and then at dusk – especially interested in low tides. Bald eagles are opportunistic hunters, seeking out stranded fish and other tidbits that low tides leave behind.

Cape Meares, near Oceanside, is known for some spectacular sights as they try and attack nests of other birds along the cliffs.

Tidepools

This is one of the most densely populated areas of the coast when it comes to tidepools. All the rocky stretches have them: Rocky Creek, Boiler Bay, and secret sections like South Point and North Point. The problem is you can't – and shouldn't – always get to them. Some, like those in Depoe Bay, are dangerous. One of the best areas is the marine gardens next to Devil's Punchbowl. See the full listings on these areas for details.

Do Not Feed the Birds or Wildlife

Yes, this is a sad thing to say and it's going to be a bummer to read. But you should not feed birds or wildlife – especially seagulls. The short of it: eating our food scraps harms them, and it makes them less frightened of humans and cars, thus endangering them even more. The other problem is that when they mass together on beaches their droppings affect water quality.

Feeding seagulls is now becoming greatly discouraged along the Oregon coast by state and local officials at a variety of levels. Cannon Beach is increasingly at the forefront of that. Various civic authorities are starting to get the word out on a wider basis, especially in towns where water quality gets affected by large flocks of birds plopping poop everywhere. Luckily, Lincoln City doesn't get hit by this too much, but most of the area is not monitored by DEQ in the first place.

Feeding seagulls is not illegal, but it is highly discouraged - and it may become illegal down the road.

To begin with, human food is bad for them. Especially the stuff that gets thrown at them more often like bread, French fries, potato chips, pizza and lunch meat. These foods have absolutely no nutritional value for gulls and can actually harm them.

Then there are the numerous traffic issues. They no longer fear cars and start to view them as big vending machines. Being highly intelligent birds they learn quickly. This is why they often don't move when you're driving through beach access parking lots.

Some fast food parking lots in particular are problematic, such as way up north in Seaside. They swarm in huge numbers there. All it takes is one French fry and you've suddenly acquired 50 birds.

Not only do the birds cause a major nuisance in terms of droppings on pavement and sheer numbers, but they get hit by other cars in the parking lot, or worse yet they wander nonchalantly into traffic on 101 and get hit there.

All hit or injured seagulls need to be euthanized. They can't be rescued or rehabilitated.

Then there are the public health issues that are the result of big flocks of seagulls. Their fecal matter gets into storm drains and hits the beach in unpleasantly large amounts. Some towns, like Cannon Beach, have had more problems with this than others. Consequently, lodgings and businesses there have been much more proactive about getting the word out to guests to "not feed the seagulls." Many lodgings in Lincoln City will declare a ban on feeding them from their patios or balconies because of the inevitable mess it leaves.

This lack of fear of vehicles has created another level of crime and vandalism as well. It gives some people more excuses to do bad things. For a time in the early 2010's, there had been numerous high profile news stories of motorists driving on beaches and killing as many as 50 seagulls at once – on purpose.

That is a crime punishable by law.

Second Summer

They call it the "second summer" on Oregon's coast and around Depoe Bay, and it's really the best time of year to hit the area for a number of reasons. There's a nice combo of weather factors that come together, providing the warmest, calmest conditions of the whole year. But you'll also find lodging prices starting to dip, less people on the roads, more beaches to yourself and often no wait times at your favorite eateries.

Less people on Lincoln County roads is a bit relative, however: there's almost always a fair amount of traffic through town.

Second summer also means the added luxury of more whale sightings.

There are exceptions, of course (like the one autumn the SOLVE Beach Cleanup had to cancel due to a freak wind storm), but you'll generally find these inviting conditions going until about the middle of October – often a bit beyond. Temps linger around 70 or more, skies are blue, and winds can be nearly nonexistent.

For decades, this was a big secret. But since about 2000 or so, the popularity of the region during this month or two has gradually increased, so that now it's not uncommon to have even weekdays be full of visitors. Those grand, inviting conditions of second summer that were once known to just a few diehards have resulted in a lot more people. Basically, the secret is out.

Some towns still see some lodging price drops after Labor Day but now it's not as much as before the early 2000s. In fact, larger towns like Seaside, Lincoln City or Newport don't drop much – if at all – until the end of September. Depoe Bay may drop a little more than others, considering its size. It doesn't always fill up as quickly as larger burghs do.

However, most weekdays boast less people amid some truly balmy weather.

Once you get to early October, then crowds and lodging prices really drop off. The second summer phenomenon is still keeping things quite warm through the middle of the month. It's about October 15 when things move towards the blustery and rainy again, although in the last fifteen years there have typically been at least a few days scattered throughout October's last two weeks that remain remarkably warm, even tropical.

Travel officials say many more two-for-the-price-of-one specials start to pop up after September 15. It's also a good time to book conferences and meetings as prices for that can be lower.

A good rule of thumb is that the more expensive the place, the more it will drop in price. Less expensive hotels or motels will drop less.

So is this Second Summer real, you're asking? The science behind it is interesting.

According to meteorologists, the valley starts to cool off in September, but meanwhile the ocean waters off the coast have heated up over summer. This lessens the temperature differences between the two areas, and this helps keep things calmer (as those differences also drive things like wind and fog during the summer). Warmer winds from the valley can make it here more easily. On top of all that, warmer air from California is allowed to come up more by that action, which warms up the Oregon coast even more.

All this lack of wind, fog and generally nicer conditions make for waves that aren't very big. That is what you need to spot whales. September and October are usually incredible for whale sightings because the wave height doesn't hide them. Calmer conditions also coax them closer to shore, where they may be checking you out as well.

In recent years, gray whale numbers have been rather high during this whole second summer thing.

Early Spring of February

There's a semi-regular occurrence each February of unusually warm weather, nicknamed the Mini Spring of February. Sure, it's winter and that's generally a time of dreary, drenching weather. But stats show there are often about 10 days of dry conditions scattered throughout February, and these can get quite warm.

It doesn't occur every year and they're not consecutive days, but some years you have a run of downright balmy days, even warmer than many parts of summer. You'll get nearly no winds and lots of sun, and that can really heat things up. Temps will soar to close 60 degrees, sometimes beyond. And with no winds, that increases how warm you feel because there is no wind chill factor.

This is especially true on the sands and the cliffs of the Depoe area. The stretches will feel much warmer, as much as 15 to 20 degrees warmer, because the sand and the ocean reflect the sun back. The temps in town can be 45 or maybe 55 degrees, and it can feel near 70 right at the tideline.

It's spectacular to encounter this.

The science behind it states that this is not all that unusual, except that on the coast, the moderate climate element can heighten the glorious weather factor.

Many areas of the United States will experience this, including inland Oregon. By this time of year, Oregon has gone through the early sunsets and the dark and wetter days. February begins to get over that hump, and the days are getting longer. That added sunlight heats up the weather just enough.

When those clear, sunny days of late winter happen – and it's not all the time, that's for certain – things are colder in the valley because of the east winds bringing colder air. In the valley it's that winter crisp: temps hovering around 40 to even freezing. On the coast, however, you can get temps more around 50, even on those near-32-degree days in the valley.

Basically, cold air settles in the valley. But on the coast, weather is automatically more moderate because it's next to the ocean, which is about 50 degrees, keeping things from straying too far away from that temperature. Even if it's raining heavily, it's often warmer on the coast than in the valley during the whole of winter, actually.

In the summer, this same element of the moderate ocean keeps the temperature down.

Again, it's important to remember this doesn't happen every year. You have to keep an eye on the weather reports. It's simply something to look out for.

Secret Spring

There's more to spring on the Oregon coast than spring break. In fact, that period after the main spring breaks - from mid April through to the end of May - is a distinctly unpopulated season with a host of interesting natural wonders that make this an unusual time of year on these beaches. It's nicknamed the "secret season," "hidden spring" or "secret spring" – various incarnations of that - because no one ever seems to talk about it. There is a growing movement of coastal businesses that are making it a point to speak up, however.

It's filled with a lot of wild wonders. From crazed sea foam, more fascinating creatures, empty beaches to really low tides and even Orcas.

Wild Weather Mood Swings. March and April bring a crazed kind of weather, often abruptly switching back and forth between sun and squalls within the same day, sometimes within a half hour. You get an interesting mix of increasingly nice days, with occasional winter-like storms still possible – periodically within the same day. May starts to calm down considerably, and you lose the big storms, but weather switch-a-roo's still happen quite often.

You'll want to come prepared for abrupt shifts in weather, bringing along changes in clothing and jackets, in case the weather decides to turn on you. In Lincoln City, you'll still have to watch those high tides during stormier days from a distance because of the width of the beaches.

Crazed Sea Foam Action. Spring storms can offer some wild, strange sights, especially when paired with the larger blooms of phytoplankton that happen this time of year. These are the microscopic creatures that whales and other fish eat in huge abundance. One kind, called diatoms, are the type of phytoplankton mostly responsible for the sea foam you see in the waves. Their millions of tiny skeletons combine with the air to make bubbles in the breakers. Basically, they make the sea foam.

With more foam because of the spring blooms, you then get a better chance of seeing sea foam pulling all sorts of strange stunts during the season's storms, like moving across the highways or even flying upwards, creating the mind-boggling sight of what looks like snow going the wrong direction.

Also see Oregon Coast Spring Surprise: Now is Most Photogenic Time of Year:
http://beachconnection.net/news/sprpho042313_623.php

Major Minus Tides. Some of the year's lowest minus tides can happen in March, April and May, with May having a tendency to be the lowest. This allows for greater exploration of tidepools at Lincoln City or Newport, but not much in the Depoe Bay area. Those colonies on rocky ledges are there pretty steadily. The tidepool wonders of Otter Rock are greatly affected by low tides, however. This is when that area is safest anyway. In fact, entire new vistas of rocky marine gardens show themselves there.

Lodging Prices Surprises. In the spring, around spring break, lodging prices start rising again after winter lows, but there's still this intermediate time where some remain at winter rates or just slightly higher. Lodging prices may even sometimes drop back down until May.

Spring lodging specials begin popping up like daisies, and that's where you can rake in the savings. Even if general rack prices don't drop back down.

Midweek savings packages are usually still around, and some inns remain 20 to 40 percent off their summer rates. See the Depoe Bay lodging page at BeachConnection.net, which features regular updates on such specials.

The Beaches Less Traveled. On top of the beautiful natural phenomena that abound this time of year, crowds are sizably less. In many beach burghs, it's almost a ghost town, even more so on the north Oregon coast. Lincoln City and Newport really empty out as does Gleneden Beach. You can enjoy the most incredible chunks of the coastline in total solitude during this "secret spring" of April and May. You're apt to find the roads and beaches completely to yourself at times, if not fairly often. This is true even on most really nice weather weekends, where things do get a bit busier – but not much so.

Orcas. Killer whales often show up in April, usually lingering through May. See the chapter about whales.

That Slippery, Dangerous Green Goo

The Depoe Bay area can carry a preponderance of that slippery green goo stuff along its rocky ledges, more so than most coastal spots. It's often dangerous to deal with, so a safety issue, but it's also beach science. Hence it's inclusion in this section of the book.

It's intriguing looking, it can be smelly, it's often very slippery and it can very easily cause you to fall on your head while on rocky areas of these beaches. The stuff is dark green, sometimes a brighter green, and it's found everywhere on these shores. Here in many sections in and around Depoe Bay, it can interfere with walking.

What is it?

We are most often looking at sea lettuce, according to Tiffany Boothe of Seaside Aquarium. The technical name is Ulva fenestrata, and Boothe said it is a green macroalgae that's distributed by the ocean from the Bearing Sea to Chile. It's actually found around the world and is composed of eight individual species.

Depending on the area, there's also seaweed, perhaps three or four different kinds. In any case, all are very slippery, often even when they're not wet.

Boothe said sea lettuce is a very important food source as it feeds a myriad of sea critters. Sea urchins, crabs, nudibranchs and even fish feed on this delicious plant.

But the surprise is you could – technically – munch on it.

"It is also consumed by humans in soups, salads, and as a substitute for nori (the popular seaweed used in preparing sushi rolls) in sushi," Boothe said. "Nutritionally, it is very healthy. Not only is it high in iron and protein, it is also packed full of vitamins and minerals. In Scotland, Ulva has become quite popular."

Boothe said sea lettuce can be found attached to hard substrates, such as pebbles, shells, or rocks, or they are free floating in calm bays and estuaries.

You'll typically find it on low-lying intertidal areas at mostly rocky beaches, like those at Haystack Rock at Cannon Beach, Yachats, Oceanside, Depoe Bay and more. You won't find it on sandy beaches like Seaside, Waldport, Newport or Lincoln City, unless there are patches of rocks that are exposed to ocean water.

The brighter green stuff may well be an algae, which is what you find at Depoe Bay's South Point. Boothe said these are likely a thing called Green Tuft (Cladophora columbiana), which is commonly found on Pacific coast beaches.

Secret But Year-round Ghost Forests of Otter Rock

When it comes to ghost forests on these shores, there's sadly a lot of misleading or incomplete information out there - on the Internet and in articles by larger media. The biggest gaffe: the Neskowin ghost forests are the only ones out there. They're the only ones ever talked about in the large, elaborate photo spreads in the state's top newspaper, and even Oregon's travel officials tout only Neskowin's stumps. Then there's the background science: that's as incomplete as can be as well.

What every visitor gets deprived of is the fact there are actually 33 locations along this entire shoreline where ghost forests might be found – from Cannon Beach down to Brookings. There are 540 documented individual stumps.

They range in age from seven thousand years to about 1,000, according to carbon dating. That work was done mostly by Oregon geologists Roger Hart and Curt Peterson in the '90s and early 2000s, for the Oregon Department of Geology and Mineral Industries.

Granted, Neskowin is the main area where these can be seen year-round. The majority are only visible when sand levels have been scoured out enough by winter storms. Some don't get seen for years, and during some winters most are not seen at all because of little storm wave action.

Two surreal and unsung attractions sit right around Otter Rock, one hiding in plain sight and the other lurking beneath a popular surfing spot. Both are some 4,000 years old, and their origins are nothing short of mind-blowing.

What's unusual about these is that they're two of very few on the entire coastline you can see year-round. And yet somehow no one knows about these. Near Waldport, there's a large one called Big Stump, set in a rather remote beach with no close public access.

These two around Otter Rock are really the most spectacular of the bunch that's visible throughout all seasons. They're larger and older.

One is cloistered just beneath Otter Rock, on its southern face. But the other, its twin, sits at Beverly Beach State Park, on Newport's outer edges.

They are stumps from trees roughly 4,000 years old, part of a "ghost forest" from some place on the central coast. Sometime in the late '90s, these ancient, nearly-petrified pieces of wood emerged from hiding beneath the sand when violent winter storms eroded the beaches. It may have been the first time they'd seen daylight in over 100 years. Not much is known about them.

About a year later, more violent storms ripped them both from whatever beach they had emerged from and one washed up at Spencer Creek, in Beverly Beach State Park, while the other managed to sneak its way into a tiny cubbyhole of a cove-like structure right beneath Otter Rock.

The Beverly stump now sits in the park on permanent display with signage explaining its origin. Rangers did move that one, and you'll find it at the entrance to the beach. Oregon State Parks and Recreation Department rangers talk of the other one showing up at the same time, with both having to be moved out of the way at one point.

It's unclear if tides washed the Otter Rock stump to its location, or it was OPRD rangers or other workers that helped nudge it there. No one at OPRD had an answer about this.

The one at Otter Rock is especially engaging as it just sits there with a weird spider shape, going absolutely unnoticed unless you stop and look carefully. Head down the southern steps to the bustling surfer beach and you'll find it lurking in a corner near the tideline. If you don't know what you're looking at, you're simply going to think it's an unusual bit of driftwood.

Periodically, it's not even accessible because of crazy tides, and the only way you can spot it is by looking down at the beach from the viewpoint above, peering into the mini cove.

How did these ghost forests come to be?

Essentially, they were swallowed up by sand at some point thousands of years ago and thus cut off from oxygen and its decaying effects on wood. Whatever did this to the forests happened fairly quickly.

Currently, Oregon geologists tend to be divided into two camps on that theory. At least depending on the locale. One theory says it happened over several years to a few decades as the landscape simply changed. The other theory is more ominous, stating that a major earthquake – like the one in 1700 – abruptly dropped the beach and surrounding ground ten or more feet.

It's largely agreed the Neskowin ghost forest is likely from a catastrophe of that sort. What happened here in Newport, Seal Rock and up on the north coast isn't as clearly defined. However, the prevailing theory for the crusty stumps near Cannon Beach is spearheaded by local geologist Tom Horning, who believes many of those up north were the result of a slower change.

Again, this is where travel officials, some high-profile journalists and certainly one major Oregon travel site (that's already known for factual errors or misleading angles) get it wrong: they consistently point to the cataclysm theory. This is partially because they're focused only on Neskowin, but there's also a lot of sloppy reporting or just downright rewriting of material from the net.

Peterson and Hart wrote a paper on the subject back in 2006, and said each of these forests were already quite ancient when they were sucked beneath sand.

"The age of the largest preserved stumps, established by counting annular growth rings, demonstrates forest soil development and tree growth for a minimum of 200 years prior to burial in the Lincoln, Neskowin and Netarts littoral cells," the paper said.

"Littoral cells" refers to the areas between headlands, and in this case means the ghost forests found at Neskowin, near Cape Lookout, Oceanside, and near Newport were at least 200 years old when they died. The oldest of the ghost stumps met their fate about 7,000 years ago, found around Bandon. while most others happened between 4,000 and 1,000 years ago, according to Hart and Peterson.

The pair largely look to the theory of a slower forest burial, rather than the earthquake-driven idea. But one of the most important components in their preservation had to be wet sand, as the scientists talked about finding "forest litter" with the trees – bits and pieces of bark, peat and other stuff you find on the ground of any forest.

"New evidence of rapid burial of preserved tree limbs on buried stumps and intact forest litter on shore platforms indicates that rapid sand accumulation played a key role in killing the forests," the paper said.

Another section of their paper discusses the fact stumps found under dry dunes decomposed more:

"The shore platform stumps are better preserved than the terrace margin stumps. These relations suggest that wet sand played an important role in the preservation of wood. Unlike stumps rooted on poorly drained shore platforms, stumps buried under drained Holocene dunes have apparently decomposed by oxidative degradation. "

Ghost Forests of Moolack Beach

Immediately south of Beverly Beach and Otter Rock - really the northern edges of Newport - Moolack Beach is the big place where ghost forests tend to pop up a little more often than others in winter. Down near Seal Rock is another spot that's often reliable for these during that season, but Moolack's you can sometimes see from the roadway.

It happens when storms slice open the beaches here, scouring out enough sand that craggy bedrock more than 22 million years old appears, along with 4,000-year-old ghost forests.

There are numerous such stumps at Moolack Beach lurking beneath those sands. The fascinating tidbit about these is that you'll notice they're primarily octopus-like shapes, essentially just root systems. That's because apparently someone here raided these for the wood, chopping them up. No one knows when this happened. It could've been decades ago.

Specimens at Neskowin were not chopped up, as well as just about all the others you periodically find, such as those at Cape Lookout State Park, Seal Rock and Arch Cape.

All those surreal rocky slabs at Moolack are made up largely of mudstone, and part of the 22 million-year-old Nye Mudstone formation, showing as olive-gray mudstone and siltstone, which weather into colors like a rusty brown. Fish scales and other tiny bits of fossils have been found here.

Unusual Sights – Rarities in General

You haven't lived until you've made at least one really weird and stunning discovery along the Oregon coast. These can happen anywhere along this shoreline: glowing sand, double-headed sunsets, the famed Green Flash at Sunset and gobs more. Some are extremely rare, some are just fairly rare.

Glowing Sand. It's often mislabeled as "phosphorescence." However, glowing sand is actually the result of tiny, bioluminescent forms of phytoplankton – meaning they glow in the same way fireflies do. What you see is a faint display of bluish / green sparks beneath your feet if you're walking in the wet sand at night. If you're lucky, it can almost look like a glow stick erupting for a few seconds, or it can show itself as a small, exploding galaxy beneath your feet if you stomp on a pool of water that's been around awhile.

You need a very dark beach to see this, one with little to no light interference. Lucky for you, Gleneden Beach and Lincoln Beach come with plenty of dark beaches. Lincoln City is also a great area to find this sparkly phenomenon.

Find more at www.BeachConnection.net on the subject.

Green Flash at Sunset. It's somewhat rare to extremely rare and it is one of the more coveted experiences. It's called the Green Flash at Sunset. The absolute right conditions have to be present. What you'll see is a brief green blob directly above the sun, just before the last sliver dips below the horizon. "Flash" is a bit of a misnomer as it tends to linger for at least a couple of seconds, sometimes nearly ten seconds. Every once in awhile, it turns the entire sliver of sun a weird green.

Contrary to popular belief, it doesn't just happen on a day with no clouds, although that's generally one of only two conditions where it's possible (see Novaya Zemlya section that follows). On really clear days, it helps to be on a high cliff. The Depoe Bay area has plenty of those, especially Cape Foulweather. Otter Rock, Rocky Creek and Boiler Bay are high enough to assist in this mind-blower as well. For even more information on this and more full color photos, see www.beachconnection.net, then do a search on "green flash."

Novaya Zemlya Effect. Ever see a two-headed sunset? Or more than two? It's an unusual ocean weather phenomenon called the Novaya Zemlya effect, and it's considered quite a rarity around the rest of the world. But it may actually be more common on the Oregon coast, making this a rather special place.

This effect creates an illusion where it seems the sun is setting later than it really is. The upper part is often distorted in appearance, most of the time showing as a series of lighted bands across the sky. Yet you always see at least part of the real orb just below, descending down towards the horizon.

In the simplest terms, it's a kind of polar image mirage of the sunset.

Interestingly, since it works on many of the same scientific principles as the green flash, it can cause a green flash at sunset. Don't forget to look closely if you see this happening at the end of a pristine, calming day: you may have just doubled your chances of seeing the coveted green lighting effect. For even more information on this and more full color photos, see www.beachconnection.net.

Singing Sands. This actually happens mostly on two spots on the coast: in some areas of the National Dunes Recreation Area south of Florence and maybe - just maybe - south of Cannon Beach. Sometimes, it sounds like distant voices singing. Others, it's a bit like a violin. Then there's that elongated squishy, squeaking noise. All of it only happens under certain conditions, when two different kinds of sands grind together under the right degree of humidity.

Sorry, but all this generally happens about 100 miles to the north.

However, more frequent is the squeaking noise, and that is not necessarily limited to Cannon Beach. I've personally heard it at Gleneden Beach, Tillicum Beach near Yachats and at Manzanita before. It seems that squeak is more common to Cannon Beach and nearby Arcadia Beach, but it's certainly possible to encounter it south of there, such as at Lincoln City.

There's more on it at www.BeachConnection.net.

Meteor Showers. There are few things more amazing than being on one of this area's beaches and ledges at night and spotting a lot of meteors. Once again, you'll need clear nights, which can be challenging on the coast – but not at state park headlands like Rocky Creek or Boiler Bay. Cape Foulweather is absolutely mind-blowing after dark, if cloudless. When nights here are clear – they're astoundingly clear. The stars are bright and the ring of the rest of the galaxy is spellbinding. Even if there are no meteor showers (like the Lyrids or others that regularly happen throughout the year), stray meteors are easy to see. If you're on the beach on a clear night, make sure you spend some time looking up.

The best areas for viewing the stars is anywhere dark in this part of Lincoln County, really.

DETAILED GUIDE TO DEPOE BAY

Coming from the North: Lincoln City, Salishan, Kernville

Lincoln City is the major metropolis to the north – well, minimetropolis, anyway. Seven miles of nearly uninterrupted beaches spread from the Roads End district at the northern edge, down to the southern tip of Taft and the Siletz Bay. Along the way, take in the town's copious attractions created by humans and those created by Mother Nature. It's all essentially sandy beaches here, with a few rock structures dotting this by-the-seascape and a smattering of tidepools.

The Roads End district of Lincoln City is where the road does indeed end - and so do the city limits. It's all accessed by a major parking lot called Road End State Recreation Area, where picnic tables and lovely views abound.

South of there, accesses like NW 40th and the Grace Hammond beach access are gateways to more sandy pleasantries, giving way to a stretch of cliffs where there are no entrances to the beach. This leaves a long stroll your only means to explore those areas – and thus find yourself out of sight of most people.

Heading south you eventually come to long stairway accesses like NW 26th and 21st, which are well worth it. The NW 15th Street entrance allows you to drive on the beach a tiny ways, and there are some nifty tidepools there.

At the center of town, the D River Wayside is probably the most populated, but comes with an enormous parking lot and those cool telescope thing-a-ma-bobs. South of there, you encounter another clifftop drive with almost no direct beach entrance until the Nelscott area and SW 35th. See the Lincoln City book in this series, as this directs you to a host of insanely cool secrets on this stretch. The Siletz Bay and the Taft district are the next big beachy attractions.

As you leave southern Lincoln City you'll slowly wander past a wildlife refuge and a tiny community called Kernville, which hosts a building once used in the "Sometimes a Great Notion" movie.

Salishan and Salishan Spit

After this tree-lined wilderness tract, you come to the community of Salishan. A famous hiking spot and an upscale business complex are the two main features here. Oh, and there is a golf course.

If you're a hotel guest or a resident of the gated community, you have access to the beach from here. Otherwise, the northernmost beach access that allows you to hike the spit is down in Gleneden

Beach quite a ways. Hiking Salishan is about an eight-mile round trip, past mostly dunes, some wildly indulgent homes and plenty of wildlife. If you're lucky enough to be a guest that shaves off about 1.5 miles from your trek. Otherwise, it's much longer.

Immediately south of here, Gleneden Beach Loop veers off from the highway into forested business districts and neighborhoods with junctions to 101 at either end. The southernmost end lies at the entrance to the state park.

Gleneden Beach

This tiny community south of Lincoln City (about five miles, if you're keeping count) has a smattering of restaurants, a community hall and sporadic vacation rentals, but no real hotel.

The real attraction is simply the beach – and it's a curious set of beaches too. Often, there's a rather steep slope to the tide line, which causes the waves to come in hard and noisy then stop quite quickly. It's a bit freaky at first. It feels like it's going to be dangerous, but it's not.

Under normal conditions, that is. Because of this – and the fact there's nothing but cliffs behind you – the area gets rougher than other beaches in storms. It's small and you can't run away from the raging tides. Use extreme caution if tides are high or the area is rather stormy. During storms, simply stay off this beach. People have died here thinking they're OK.

Also notable about these beaches is the proliferation of larger, coarser sand grains, and some tracts of blackish sands. These are always determined by the geology of the surrounding area. Just about every beach has a different composition.

History of Gleneden Beach

The origins of Gleneden Beach go back well before the 1920s, according to the North Lincoln County History Museum. A family of immigrants from Poland settled here first, with the last name Sijota. There's still a street by that name in the little village. As the only residents in the area, the village was originally called Sijota.

According to the museum's Jeff Syrop:

"The area was remote, even for coastal towns. Because schools of the day were far from the Sijota homestead, Mrs. Sijota started a school in her home."

At some point in the 1920s, a Mr. and Mrs. William F. Cary bought a large parcel of land from the family, and formed a business called Siletz Investment Company to sell residential and vacation home lots.

The couple had two daughters by the name of Glen and Phyllis. When they got the chance to pick a name for the area for themselves, they chose Gleneden, based on the name of one daughter and the idea of "Eden," something suggestive of a kind of paradise. A little while later "Beach" was added to the name for marketing purposes, making for Gleneden Beach.

North Lincoln County History Museum records show that by 1927, Gleneden Beach had about 225 lots, a water department and a post office. Highway 101 – called the Roosevelt Highway then – was created a year earlier but had not been surfaced yet when the town began to take shape.

"There was no bridge over the Siletz River, so the town was still hard to reach," Syrop said.

Hidden Access of Gleneden Beach

Off Gleneden Beach Loop, a couple of streets will lead you to beach entrances, including your best bet for accessing Salishan Spit because of the locked gate farther north.

Wander west down Sijota St. until you reach Neptune St. and a hidden access there. Miles and miles of fluffy sand await you. This is the northernmost access towards the Spit.

From this access, it's a three-mile hike south to Fishing Rock.

Another small access sits a few streets south near Easy St. Yes, that's its real name. That one has trouble with erosion, and you may occasionally find the slope eroded and a bit of a steep descent and ascent. There has been a metal stairway on and off over the years; sometimes it's simply gone. You can see by the picture here: one year in the mid 2010s it had been visibly been beaten up.

Gleneden Beach State Recreation Area

Near milepost 122, a ways after Lincoln City and the Salishan area, and just before you get to the Lincoln Beach area, sits this gem of a state park.

A large parking lot allows for plenty of beachgoers, but during slower seasons you'll find yourself largely alone at Gleneden Beach State Recreation Area. Picnic tables, a small lawn area, and a picnic shelter for groups are also highlights on this grass-covered plot above the beach. There are restrooms aplenty as well.

One of the treats here is a sort of defacto lookout point at the end of the road next to the parking lot. The cliff here has started to fall apart, but you can still hang out just beyond the barriers and look down on the surf. This is particularly satisfying at night, when you can stop at the edge and shine your headlights down there, and then sit back and take in the nocturnal surf show.

Descend down a fairly short path, through a thick forested stretch, and you'll find the opening to this magnificent and rather unique beach. It's all sand here – and comprised of coarse, large sand granules as well. Yellow sandstone cliffs in one state of crumbling or another also add to the atmosphere. These really light up at sunset: don't forget your camera.

Walk a ways to the north and you'll start encountering the backstreet neighborhoods and hidden accesses of Gleneden Beach. Walk south and you'll quickly enter Lincoln Beach. Within a mile, this beach then dead-ends at the point known as Fishing Rock. To the north, it keeps going for miles until you reach the end of the Salishan Spit.

Gleneden Beach State Recreation Area and Lincoln Beach are popular areas for surfers.

Another fascinating aspect of this area is the steep tideline. Parts of Lincoln City have this, but here the sand forms a much steeper rise next to the ocean – instead of a gradual rise you have at most beaches. The result is a dynamic where waves come slamming in rather fast and hard, but dissipate in power quite quickly. It's alarming and disconcerting at first, but once you get used to it you'll find it a kick in the pants.

The sand itself in this area is always a bit curious as well. It's comprised of the usual whiter, softer sands, but in spots it's mixed in with courser, darker granules. So you get chunks where the sand darkens a bit and feels rougher to the skin.

Hence, there are even more colors and moods to Gleneden Beach.

Aside from its disposition during the day, after dark it has a sublime beauty as well. Depending on the sky conditions, the stars can open up to reveal some intense galactic vistas, or cloud cover or fog make for wild displays as various light sources bounce through the atmosphere.

Lincoln Beach

This tiny community between Depoe Bay and Gleneden Beach is where the commercial district begins and Highway 101 gives way to two lanes. It comes with a lot of the needed amenities of civilization, such as a grocery store, coffee and an eatery or two.

Lincoln Beach sits a mile south of Gleneden Beach and about two miles north of Depoe Bay. Like Gleneden Beach, this stretch is often full of coarser, larger grains of sand and steep tidelines.

A couple of tiny, barely-marked beach accesses sit amid the neighborhoods.

Wallace St. Access

It's the final access of Lincoln Beach – just look for Wallace St. and follow it to its end. This is an interesting one, with rather intricate cliffs, some giant blob rocks to break up the scenery, and one really weather-beaten tree that's somewhat remarkable.

Storms don't bode well for this place, but you're in luck: a gravel area lets you watch the wild waves in safety from your car. They seriously put on a show here, but it's too crazy to walk on the beach at times like that. In short, this is a great storm watching spot.

Fishing Rock State Recreation Site

As the Lincoln Beach area ends, a tad north of milepost 125, one of the Oregon coast's more engaging secret spots sits hiding almost in plain sight. If you blink along this two-lane stretch of passing and hustle and bustle, you'll miss it.

Part of the Oregon State Parks system, Fishing Rock State Recreation Site lies tucked away, just out of sight enough to not be a crowded destination – but still with a fervent following to keep it slightly abuzz. It's also one of the smallest of the state parks, but big on surprises.

What stands out here are the wild colors of the cliffs, the craggy, rocky basalt edges that form mesmerizingly cool structures to climb around on, and a variety of large-scale and miniature viewpoints that are always cause for dropping of the jaw.

If you're looking for something a little different on your next coastal trip, this is it. Some place you haven't been before, and one that not quite everyone knows about. Here, you can feel like you're part of the in-crowd, in a beachy way.

There isn't much that alerts you to the existence of this uncompromisingly unique little chunk of coastal cliffs. Sure, there's a sign along this part of Highway 101 that says "Fishing Rock State Recreation Site," but there's no visual clue what that's about. You'll see an RV park on one side and a smattering of dwellings on the seaward side, but the park itself sits a few hundred feet back and out of sight.

So let the curiosity get the better of you and meander down that small, gravelly road. You'll come to a small gravel parking lot, with a fence that gives it an old West corral vibe.

First, you have to get through the labyrinth-like path cut through thick, otherwise impenetrable brush. Even that looks a bit confusing as still no ocean views from here. A thick rainforest vibe envelops you, but you start to hear the ocean. This place knows how to build the excitement.

Don't be fooled by the other trails wiggling in and around the thick brush: you'll just get lost. They usually dead-end rather quickly.

Eventually you exit the green to wondrous views, where even in the calmest conditions the ocean explodes in endless configurations of watery pyrotechnics. The basalt rocks of Fishing Rock State Scenic Recreation Site jut out into the sea and don't allow for any gradual rise of the tideline, creating a constant barrier to the power of the Pacific. With nowhere else to go but up, the waves knock around, splash about and create a constant raucous.

When larger storms come, the place is wilder and more violent than any Hollywood action flick.

This tiny headland is quite a mix of grassy stretches, soft sandstone-like soil and bumpy rock features.

Look down and westward from the tip of the main section and the really mesmerizing show begins: odd, pockmarked rock structures of varying shades of beige mixed with bubbly basalts and odd knobs populate this place. This is where much of the major splashing is conducted. There are a smattering of basalt objects to climb around on – but be extremely careful not to go too far as it's easy to wind up in a place where the ocean wallops the basalt. Those waves may pounce on you and take you down.

To the left (or south), you see a mysterious cove, filled with funky black sands of unusually large proportions. That spot beckons to you even more because there is no way down there. Not that you could survive for long if you did. The ocean prefers covering it up completely most of the time.

A bit further south lie the headlands that house Fogarty Creek State Recreation Site and beyond that even Whale Cove. But you can't see any of those, Instead, more rough seas are visible from here at almost any time of the year. More splashing against jagged, black shapes. More oceanic monsters firing up in the air.

 Look north and you're staring down and out along the vast expanse of Lincoln Beach as it slowly morphs into Gleneden Beach.

There is a portion of these rocks that does let you amble down to Lincoln Beach when tidal conditions allow, and vice versa: you can climb up to Fishing Rock from Lincoln Beach. But much of the time that's not a good idea, so take a good note where the tides are. You could get stuck walking almost a mile to the nearest beach access to get up to 101 and then the same distance to get back to where you're parked.

Another section of the trail skirts along the cliffs and takes you southward a little bit, where you can look back at the fenced viewpoints of the headland.

Fogarty Beach State Recreation Area

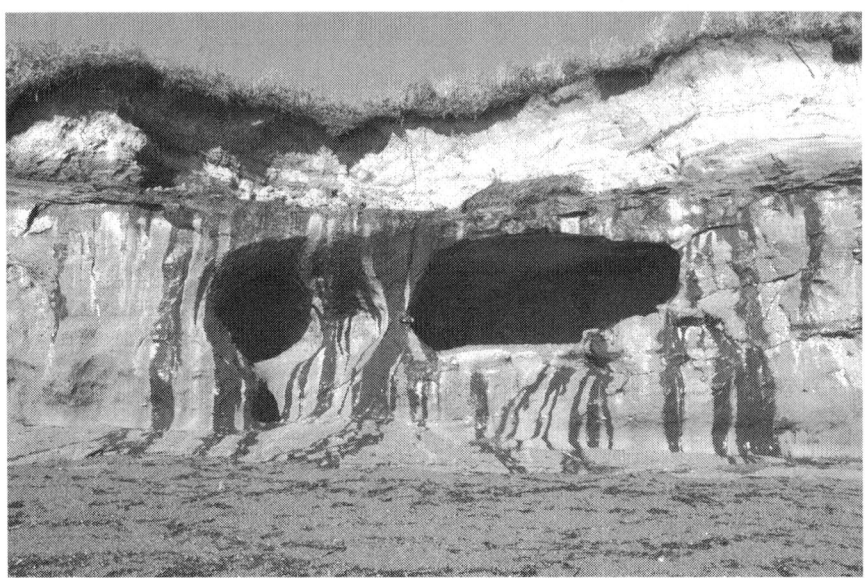

A popular place by most any standards, it's a central Oregon coast hotspot that still has a bit of a secretive vibe to it. Fogarty Beach State Recreation Area manages to coax in hundreds a day during the bustling times of the year, and yet there is still a lot about it that's relatively unknown by many.

Fogarty Beach, with calming Fogarty Creek cutting right through it, is a spot full of wonders both subtle and standing in plain view. You start out trudging through a thick forest canopy that hides a few nooks and crannies of its own. Make sure you spend a bit of time exploring the trees at some point.

The wooded surroundings quickly give way to the creek and a passage under Highway 101, and then the wonders begin – again. If the area is misty at all, you're in for some fine visual nuggets, such as the sunlight traversing through layers and branching out into a variety of colors. This is especially lovely along the stream.

Immediately, you'll notice the unusual nature of the sands here. They are enormous grains, often like tiny rocks. This makes walking barefoot a bit uneasy and flip-flops an exercise in patience as you're forced to constantly shake out the larger chunks. In short, it's pretty ouchy.

Head to the left and encounter the large blob rock that dominates the view from much of Fogarty Beach. Here, the storm waves can get impressive, leaping into the air with ferocity as they hit the basalt. That's when you have to settle for viewing it from afar, however.

The northern side of this miniature cove gets awfully rough when waves get big, but don't even bother with the entire beach during actual storms. This place can get truly hazardous.

In calmer conditions, however, the right (northern) half of the beach is an engaging half circle where really interesting stuff is found.

Among the highlights: those large holes in the cliffs. Technically, they're caves, but really small ones. Unfortunately, they sit too high to climb in. Even so, you would want to stay out of them in case the cliff decides it doesn't like you and starts caving in. This is softer sandstone, after all.

When sand levels get low, look closely at the weird, almost alien rock shapes scattered around. Some truly awe-inspiring little surprises lurk in the surf here.

A totally secret beach sits on the other side of the rocks at the far northern end, close to the cave-like holes. This is the cove beneath Fishing Rock State Recreation Area, the area almost always covered in swirling, angry tides. On rare occasions, this beach becomes briefly accessible. Very rarely, however.

Exploring That Secret Beach

Every once in awhile – mostly in summer when sand levels get super high and the ocean calms down – you can get access to that secret beach. Do NOT attempt this unless there's plenty of room between the tideline and that rocky point that separates you from Fogarty. Luckily, there's normally way too much tidal action to even get near the rocky point much less get around it. So, yes there's a lot of danger, but it's usually a case of either / or when it comes to accessibility. Either you can access it or you can't. And usually you cannot.

This rather esoteric little cove-like stretch of large sands is indeed a fascinating one, however. So let this serve as a record for you if you can't get there.

The spot is only a couple hundred feet long, and its width, even on a tranquil day, is tiny. If there are any even small sneaker waves you'd be in trouble. As you wander towards the long, finger-like outcropping of Fishing Rock, the cliff always closely hugs the shoreline. It slowly changes from an odd slate gray to the sandstone and softer sediments much of the central Oregon coast is known for.

Immediately after the blob rocks that guard its entrance, there is a little hole burrowed into the cliff by the batterings of the tide. Funky mini-caves like this abound throughout this secret spot, sometimes lurking in high places.

In another section, there's a tiny but actual sea cave hiding inside a big groove in the cliffs. From outside it's dark and slightly foreboding, and frankly it probably wouldn't be high enough or safe enough to enter.

As you wander close to this secret beach's edge you encounter a private entrance or two. At the end of this tiny cove are more of those large, coarse grains of sand which can acquire quite a sheen under blue skies.

Odd Facts: Mysterious Shapes at Fogarty Beach

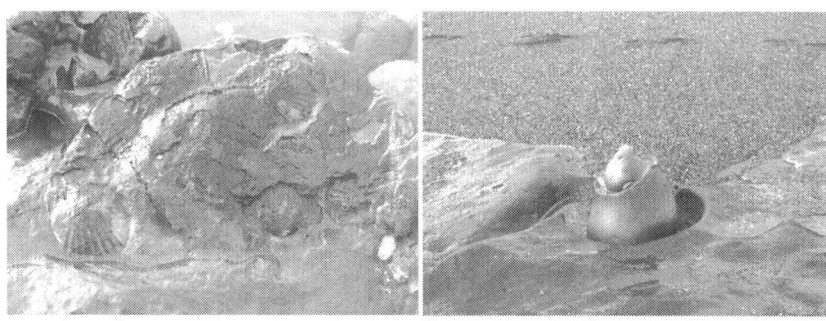

Some truly weird and astounding stuff lurks beneath the sands of Fogarty Beach. The catch: you'll only find them in winter – and even then not every winter.

These unusual sights show up very rarely: only when sand levels get scoured out by winter storms to extremely low levels. Jagged grooves show when the bedrock here is uncovered. Wild fossils lurk in the rocks (some of which are even viewable when sand levels are in the more normal range). And then there are some objects almost impossible to describe.

Sometimes there are massive grooves in the bedrock of Fogarty Beach, as seen in early 2007. During that winter – and the following one – sand levels got so low that all kinds of things were uncovered.

These have an interesting explanation, according to local experts like Guy DiTorrice, Laura Joki of Lincoln City agate shop Rock Your World, and geologist Jonathan Allan, Ph.D, with the Oregon Department of Geology and Mineral Industries.

Both Allan and Joki agreed the bedrock is of the Astoria formation, which is about 15 to 20 million years old. This part of it is mudstone, and the grooves are what geologists term "rills" which have been eroded into this rock.

According to Allan:

"This occurs through a variety of approaches, including wave action (oscillatory currents), abrasion (especially when sand levels that periodically cover the platforms fall below 30 cm, the sand begins to act as an abrasive), cavitation (hydraulic effects), and wetting/drying cycles (exposure to sun). Biological effects can also contribute to some of this."

In other words, it's a combo of waves digging at it, the sand grinding into it, and changes in how dry or wet the rock is. He's also indicating there's less than a foot of sand that normally covers Fogarty Beach.

Then there's that truly unique object that looks like an egg. Joki and Allan say it's a "concretion," something built up very slowly over time.

"The light thing sticking out of the darker rock is a concretion, a rock formed around old dead things that died and sunk to the bottom of the ancient ocean," Joki said. "Sometimes there are fossils in the concretions, sometimes not."

Allan said concretions form through various chemical reactions.

"Essentially they form by the precipitation of mineral cement within the spaces between particles," Allan said.

These can be found in sedimentary rock or soil.

Then there is that touch of Jurassic Park at Fogarty, with the fossil of a large scallop called a petcin. It too is around 15 to 20 million years old, Allan and Joki said. They are the ancient relatives of the sea scallops we know today.

When sand levels get low around here you may see different things uncovered. What happens underneath the sands – in terms of new concretions or formations – can be different year to year. You'll still see the same fossils, of course.

An important note: it is absolutely illegal to dig fossils out of a cliff or bedrock in Oregon.

Boiler Bay Gravel Viewpoint

Continue south from Fogarty Beach and you'll be covered in a thick coastal forest on either side of 101. Then within a mile you'll come to a gravel pullout with no markings, right at a rather tight curve in the road. Blink and you'll miss it.

This is probably for good reason. There's a trail down to one portion of Boiler Bay but it's not always advisable to go down there. But if you do, make sure conditions are 100 percent calm and the tide isn't anywhere near the rocks below – that there's plenty of space between the tideline and the rocky cliff. Over the last three decades, several visitors to the Oregon coast have lost their lives here.

Not for the physically weak, it takes a bit out of you to gain access to the tidal intrigue scattered around here. A small gravel parking lot at the top leads to a rather steep and boulder-laden trail snaking its way down to the bay. At higher tides there's very little beach here, and even at lower tides it's mostly a labyrinth of rocky slabs and stones, sometimes covered with that nasty, green algae that'll make you slip and fall on your head in a split second.

However, the fun of Boiler Bay lies in its awesome tidepools, clandestine caves and meandering paths over and around its mostly rocky landscape. If the tide is low enough, there's an endless array of exploration to be had, opening up tiny coves and other places to hide from the world.

The bay is named after its ancient, ragged resident: the boiler from the shipwrecked J. Marhoffer, which settled here after catching fire at sea. The boiler is all that remains, and it becomes visible at somewhat lower tides. In fairly rare circumstances, the tide gets low enough to get near the boiler or maybe even touch its encrusted corpse.

Getting back up is a strenuous climb, and for those unwilling or unable to make the jaunt there's picnic facilities and plenty of magnificent views from the parking lot.

Secret Part of Oregon Coast Trail

As you park at the gravel pullout of Boiler Bay, you may notice a nondescript little sign that says Oregon Coast Trail. Continue down this path for some remarkable secrets. It's part of the Boiler Bay to Fogarty Creek portion of the Oregon Coast Trail, running just over a mile before it meets up with Fogarty Beach at the northern end.

It's not intentionally a secret, but as of this writing even the Oregon State Parks and Recreation Department's Oregon Coast Trail website has nothing on it. According to OPRD, it is quite a new trail.

This is a magical hidden stretch, partially because of the tremendous views here and partially because of the rather mystical vibe this thickly forested path exudes.

Upon first entering, you're absolutely enveloped by dense

greenery. Giant old trees abound, some of which are just massive, craggy and broken up stumps now. Some look as if they have big, spooky faces – hence the mystic feeling.

There's only a couple of breaks in the brush here, which gleefully let you look down on Boiler Bay, including parts you didn't even know existed. At the farthest south lookout, you're actually closer to the old boiler than you can get any other way.

Major words of caution: stay a good five, six feet back from the edges of these openings, as they're clearly sitting on mushy ground that has given way in the past. You just don't know how stable these are. In the case of rainy weather, especially if the soil has been soaked for some time, stay farther back from the edge. OPRD is quick to point out these are not officially part of the trail and they too urge caution.

After the first two or three lookouts, that's about it for the viewpoints along this hiking trail. You can hear the ocean and the highway (as it skirts fairly close to 101), but you can't really see the waters the rest of the way north. A lot of public utility work was done about 2016, which opened up the forest a lot, allowing for some visibility of the highway farther north, but not the ocean.

At the Fogarty Beach side, you'll find the access on the southeast portion of the state park. A set of rocky steps brings you up to the trail and a bit more of a rise, which some say makes this a moderate hike rather than an easy one as some hiking sources have classified it. The hike is quite flat to the south, however.

As part of the Oregon Coast Trail, this allows hikers to dodge the highway for a little while. However, the highway is the only route for about two miles between here and Depoe Bay, when sidewalks take over.

Another major highlight of this little trail: it is the entrance to a very secret beach.

If you've ever been on the main headland of Boiler Bay State Scenic Viewpoint and looked north across the bay at a mysterious cobblestone beach, you've probably thought the only souls who can access this are those from the exclusive gated community over there. It turns out, there is an entrance way from this trail.

It's actually a muddy, brush- and log-covered slope that appears near the trail's entrance, and it's a bit hard to see. Getting down there is not easy, either: you'll often find it rather slippery and goopy in spots, and it's entirely possible that during rainier stretches you won't even be able to traverse it because of a steady runoff that's zipping downward.

While not necessarily dangerous it's pretty rough, but worth the strain. While the beach itself is small and kind of annoying to walk on (those polished rocks and thick sands don't make for easy going), there are some intriguing rock features here.

Boiler Bay State Scenic Viewpoint

The headland is actually the main attraction. Part of the state park system, there is a lot going on here. Some of this sprawling, grass-covered treasure contains a few nooks and crannies that are a bit hard to find. It is powerfully scenic, with equally powerful waves rumbling past.

Restrooms, picnic tables and plenty of stunning views abound here. A nice, long lawn-like area provides a slightly pastoral experience as you take in the ocean air, and maybe walk your dog a tad. Lined with a rustic log fence, you can lean over just a bit and take in a tiny splash of ocean mist on your face from these fairly rambunctious waves.

Take a look straight out westward and watch the waves smack the basalt rocks, sometimes with a fury. They can really fire into the air here.

Look southward and soak up the sights of Depoe Bay as more waves slam into the rocks on the headland's southern face. The ocean puts on a real show here as well.

Point yourself to the north and that is Boiler Bay – the whole bay. Much of it is a vast space full of rolling waves of varying ferocity. But chunks of the stony structures close to the headland have curious shapes: a series of bulbous blobs and knobby features that look just a little alien.

Other, slightly more mysterious areas lie at the bay's very northern edge – places you apparently can't go. Oh, but it turns out you can. See the previous listing. That small beach simply screams pirates' treasure.

At night, Boiler Bay State Scenic Viewpoint is still astounding. Once your eyes adjust, those ferocious waves take on a more surreal and ethereal look, even ghostly, with the lights of Gleneden Beach and Lincoln City completing the effect.

Exploding Ship Near Depoe Bay: How Boiler Bay Got Its Name

On Wednesday, May 18, 1910, the steam schooner J. Marhoffer was en route to Astoria from San Francisco, passing by what would later become Depoe Bay (apparently still called Depot Bay then). About 3 p.m. (or 4 p.m., depending on the article), a fire broke out in the engine room, caused by first assistant engineer James Kane and a gasoline soldering torch he was using.

What resulted was a major explosion which enveloped the engine room. There was not enough time to shut off the steam, according to a Newport newspaper at the time called the Yaquina Bay News. Miraculously, Kane wasn't injured in the explosion. Some of the 20 crewmen rushed to scene with fire fighting equipment but to no avail. Captain Gustave Peterson ordered everyone into the lifeboats, realizing the entire ship was ready to explode.

The ship was still about four miles out to sea.

All 20 of the crew, the captain and his wife raced to the aft of the ship to where the boats were, but quickly encountered a veritable furnace as well as choking smoke. After all, this section was where the fire was, one deck below. To make things worse, the ship was racing ahead at full speed. The largest of the two boats was lowered first, containing three men. It encountered a series of failures dropping into the ocean and was clipped by part of the vessel, causing it to capsize. The three were able to cling to the boat until they were rescued later on.

The second boat launched more successfully, containing the rest of the crew, the captain and his wife.

Her name is oddly left out of all the accounts, and she's only referred to as Mrs. Peterson. A larger article by the Yaquina Bay News at the time has a whole section devoted to her bravery and guidance during the ordeal. It says she "was the calmest and coolest person among the ships company: and the composure she exhibited with grim death staring her in the face – death by roasting alive, being blown up or drowning – her example stimulated, encouraged and moved every member of the crew and excited their admiration."

The last man off the ship was the chief engineer, who scooped up the ship's bulldog, which had been thrown overboard earlier.

After a time, the second boat managed to make it back to where the first one had capsized, and crews managed to right it. Survivors then divided themselves between the two boats and headed for shore, searching for a place to land. Twilight was hitting by the time they made it to Fogarty Beach, then simply known as Fogarty Creek or Big Cove.

One of the men rescued from the capsized boat was the cook, Frank Tiffney. He was suffering from exposure and exhaustion and died onshore. Tiffney was the only casualty among the 22; or 23 crew members if you're counting the dog.

Meanwhile, the abandoned steamer was still rushing towards shore and essentially went bonkers with no one to pilot it. Shortly before crashing, it did a full circle in the ocean extremely close to shore. Just then, its tanks exploded and threw burning oil onto trees on the bluff above its future resting place (called Briggs Landing then). It was that near to land. A few minutes later it finally plowed into the rocks.

A few more minutes later, after burning so intensely, the J. Marhoffer broke in two. More explosions and fires occurred, and the flames were reportedly seen from miles in either direction as darkness fell. The aft section stayed, thus leaving the boiler. The front end eventually drifted off, and photos of its resting place look like Nye Beach of old, or more likely Moolack or Beverly Beach.

Survivors of the vessel had found themselves on land, where the cook died. They had no other clothes than what was on their backs and no provisions, so many of them went different directions in search of help. Being a very sparsely populated section of Oregon back then, most found nothing and returned to the landing site to at least keep close to a warm fire.

The captain, his wife and first officer Johnson happened upon a cabin in the dark, finding it unoccupied. They broke in and spent the night, stumbling out in the morning to eventually find a farm owned by the Chatterton family. At their homestead the trio were fed breakfast, then set out again – apparently heading south.

Chief engineer Hastorf managed to find the road to Newport in the pitch black, eventually leading him to the Yaquina Head Lighthouse and its crew sometime in the morning. One of the lighthouse keepers, a man named Wilson, took a team on foot towards the shipwrecked crew and bumped into the captain, his wife and the first officer. He walked them back to Newport.

Meanwhile, some of the Chatterton family and their neighbors, the Greenwoods, made a sizable feast with coffee and walked it all down to Fogarty Creek where the rest of the crew were huddled.

Hastorf had walked up to the Life Saving Station in Newport and reported the wreck to officials there – what would eventually become the Coast Guard. A crew from that station, along with Hastorf, went back towards the wreck, grabbing Captain Peterson along the way, with the whole bunch reaching the landing site around 1 p.m. Glad to see the men scarfing down all the free food, the captain and some of the station team went back up to Briggs Landing (currently known as Boiler Bay) to see if anything could be salvaged. They found only a charred chunk of useless metal and no materials of any use.

Later that afternoon, the county coroner, Dr. FM Carter, came to investigate the death of Tiffney. He found that "Tiffney had come to his death through fright, chill and exposure for which no one was in any way responsible," the Yaquina Bay News writes.

Tiffney is buried in Newport still, alongside the graves of other sailors lost in the area, including the steamer Minnie F Kelton that had wrecked right around Boiler Bay just two years before.

According to another article by the paper, within a day or two of the event, three local men by the name of Corgan, Davies and Walker drove down to that cove around 1 p.m. and rigged sails onto the two lifeboats, setting out to sea with them in a salvage effort.

"One of the boats arrived at the whistling buoy off the mouth of the bay at 3 o'clock, beating the second boat by an hour" the newspaper goes on to say. "At 9 o'clock they arrived here, sailing the entire distance of sixteen miles on the ocean and fourteen miles up the bay. They report a pleasant trip although a heavy sea was running. One of the boats will be used as a tender and life boat for the steamer Truant."

The two small boats were later sold to the Modern Improvement Company of Toledo, according to a June 2 edition of the paper. The men snagged a handsome $52.50 for the salvage.

You can find more on the Marhoffer at the Lincoln County Historical Society and museum in Newport. 545 SW 9th Street, Newport, Oregon. 541-265-7509.

Northern Depoe Bay

Immediately after Boiler Bay's headland you enter the northern tip of Depoe Bay. Traffic alert: police can patrol this town with more frequency than other coastal towns, often in unmarked vehicles. Watch your speed here.

You enter a business district with plenty of condos, then about a half a mile into town you'll encounter a sidewalk with a barrier, and there's a bit of a secret viewpoint here. You can look out over the cove that spreads between the condos and the mini-headland called North Point.

Secret Access: North Point

At first glance, it's a barren, maybe even discomforting landscape, made of black, craggy and semi-smoothed-over basalt structures, all hovering above a surfline that's rather crazy no matter how calm the conditions.

That arm of black rock that stretches out from the northern edge of Depoe Bay? (If you're looking from the seawall). That's it – and it is called North Point. If it has an official name at all, that isn't completely clear. It's also a big secret of this central Oregon coast town – one spectacular stretch of clandestine cliffs that are hiding in plain sight.

You'll find a lot lurking in this slice of coastline that is perhaps a mere one eighth of a mile long, which is tucked away behind a handful of neighborhood streets at the northern end of Depoe Bay. You can't really see it from anywhere – except that part of it that juts out into view from downtown Depoe. Even the actual accesses are difficult to spot as you drive by them.

That rocky promontory that stretches out into the ocean contains another kind of spouting horn: a section of the rock seems to squeeze much of the wave action into a nearly constant spray of sea water. From this section you can look back to Depoe Bay as if you were on a boat.

Whales have been known to loiter quite close to this area, providing absolutely breathtaking encounters with a behemoth cetacean maybe within thirty feet of you. Fishermen often love this spot.

All sorts of curious structures abound here. Waves bounce off surfaces and make daring acrobatic leaps with regularity. One chunk on the northern part looks a bit like train track embedded in the basalt rock – even more startling it looks as if the train track just ends in mid air. Another small formation resembles the goofed-up replica of Stonehenge in the "Spinal Tap" flick. It too stands a few inches tall.

One of the more spectacular features of North Point is a sunken area that feels a little bit like a miniature basement, complete with steps going down that have formed naturally.

A seriously impressive feature of this spot is the weird vibrations you get under some conditions. On more temperamental days, you can actually feel the waves resonate through the basalt as they slam it. This spot is really quite unique on the coast in this respect.

This is not a good spot for stormwatching, however, or if the waves are too nutty. This rocky shelf is not an area to be trifled with or tested. Stay clear of the edge – well clear of it, as slippery spots may exist and that could still cause you to tumble down. People have been hurt here before.

Coming in handy on those crazier days, barring excessive winds, there is a grassy section above the black basalt which contains a bench and a picnic table.

How to find it? Look for Vista Ave. or Sunset Ave. at the northern edge of town and head west into that neighborhood. Be courteous and cautious here as there's not much parking and these are private homes. Look carefully for the sign that points to the cliffs: it's hard to find.

Downtown Depoe Bay

This central Oregon coast hotspot is well, almost a hotspot. Not to say that it isn't swollen with crowds and traffic during the big season or other high-density days – really even beyond capacity sometimes. But it's still a tad overlooked.

Downtown is where it all takes place: part tourist trap and part natural spectacle, and it's an irresistible and yet tranquil stop while zipping through the central Oregon coast. Depoe Bay's downtown area consists of about two or three blocks worth of businesses - an area crammed with curio shops, restaurants of all sizes and cost ranges, along with a stunning view of the ocean.

It's also where the engaging bridge resides, beneath which sits the bay, and where the famed Spouting Horn fires off with varying degrees of intensity. The Whale Watching Center is along this stretch as well.

History of Depoe Bay

According to the city's historical documentation, the name of Depoe Bay comes from a local resident. This from an online recounting created by a local resident for the city's website – a document that no longer exists:

"Evidence indicates that the first persons who were known to be actual residents of Depoe Bay were William Charles DePoe, the City's namesake, and his wife Minerva. William Charles has been described as a Siletz Indian, or due to his last name, as part French and part Indian. There seems to be no doubt that Minerva was a Siletz Indian."

Exactly how he originally spelled his name is still a controversy. But somewhere along the line the town adopted the "Depoe" spelling.

According to the North Lincoln County History Museum in Lincoln City:

"When homesteaders began settling in the area now known as Lincoln County, many Native Americans would adopt or were given English names by the settlers who could not pronounce their names. Charlie Depoe was called "Depot Charlie" (later gentrified to Depoe) because of his diligence in making sure supplies intended for the Siletz Reservation made safe passage. He and his family were allotment holders in the area we now know as Depoe Bay. Charlie Depoe was held in high esteem by homesteaders and when his heirs sold the Depoe land to the Sunset Investment Group, the town was named after him. The first post office opened in 1928 and the town officially became incorporated in 1973."

There are photos of Depoe from the 1920s showing him in full regalia.

The bay itself is referenced in 1910 by a local Newport newspaper as being called Depot Bay. This is 16 years before the land was sold from Charlie Depoe's heirs to the Sunset company – some 200 acres. For a time, like Charlie, the area was known as Depot Bay.

Purchasing of the land happened in 1926, but by some accounts the town essentially got its start around 1927 as the Roosevelt Highway came into existence here, along with the bridge. A late bloomer, it wasn't an official city until 1973, when 174 locals voted for the incorporation (and 53 voted against).

Lincoln City was just ahead of Depoe Bay's incorporation, having officially come together in 1964 out of seven little different communities, some of which were official towns and some of which weren't. Those two are rather unusual for coastal towns, since most seem to have incorporated by the 1920s.

In the mid '20s, a crowd had gathered around a dead octopus that had somehow wandered from the sea to the side of the road. This became the inspiration for the Depoe Bay Aquarium, built in 1927 by one of the city founders, H. L. Collins. It preceded even the Seaside Aquarium by a few years. The interior was filled with rock walls, which have been imitated by the Depoe Bay Winery a few doors down from the spot where the aquarium once stood.

The Depoe Bay Aquarium also featured seals, sea lions and other aquatic life, but you weren't supposed to feed these ones. There was a large oval hole in the back of the building – which is still evident today – where you could hear the seals carousing and barking. Sometimes, if you poked your head in, one of the seals would look up at you and acknowledge you with a grunt.

The aquarium survived until Labor Day weekend in 1998. The building remains, at the corner next to the north end of the bridge, at the stop light. The oval hole is now covered by glass.

Other landmarks in "downtown" are the viewpoint landing next to the Whale Watch Center, the walkway beneath the bridge, and a sort of secretive park hiding in plain sight next to the parking lot of the Tidal Raves restaurant, just north of downtown.

Whale Watch Center, Depoe Bay

Headquarters to the Whale Watch Spoken Here program that operates the twice-yearly Whale Watch Weeks, here you can hang out and learn a lot about whales as well as see them. Staff are always present to help you see whales in the Depoe Bay area. They can create quite the eye-popping display as they dive, shoot out their blowholes, spyhop and breach.

Whales migrate past here twice a year and thus the sightings greatly increase in late winter and early spring. But numerous whales loiter year-round in this area: the so-called "resident whales," hanging out to take advantage of the cove's unique feeding grounds for mycid shrimp.

Two floors exist at the Whale Watch Center: the upper floor and the bottom floor. Or you can linger outside along the seawall and spot the cetaceans, or just watch the many fishing vessels, Coast Guard craft and whale tour boats jetting in and out.

A myriad of displays about whales, seals and other sea life abound at the Whale Watch Center. You can even watch films on the subject.

Located at the southern end of the Depoe Bay Bridge, right next to the bay, on Hwy 101, Depoe Bay, Oregon. (541) 765-3407 and (541) 765-3304. www.whalespoken.org.

Depoe Bay Landmark: Spouting Horn

A large crevice in the basalt rocks of Depoe Bay near the sea wall is known to compress sea water and then fire it into the air in a spectacular, energetic display. This is the town's spouting horn – the only such blow hole within the downtown area of any

Oregon coast burgh.

This oceanic geyser can reach 40 feet or more, creating an enormous plume. It is also known to spray traffic wandering past. To say the least, it's a bit of a startling (and amusing) experience to have to turn on your windshield wipers because of an ocean wave soaking your car.

Fall, winter and heavy seas of spring are when you're most likely to catch this. It doesn't work like clockwork, so don't get upset if it's not putting on a show for you. You may find it in summer, but it's quite infrequent that time of year. Higher tides, no matter the general conditions, can cause it. But it's mostly a combo of heavier wave action and higher tides.

Locals and businesses living near the bridge and sea wall have to wash their cars and properties with frequency because of the constant spray of sea mist from the spouting horn. It even soaks buildings well across the street, as far as a block up the hill. It's not uncommon to leave your car in one of the parking areas on that incline – or certainly one of the motels nearby – and come back to find your vehicle fairly crusty from salt water. That mist is like Superman: leaping tall buildings and getting everywhere.

About Spouting Horn Safety: it should go without saying that wandering beyond the sea wall is a bad idea, especially into the vicinity of the spouting horn. This is, after all, where the waves are at their wildest.

Poking Around Pillow Basalt of the Oregon Coast

The shorelines of Oregon are filled with a huge variety of beach environments, from sandy and fluffy to rocky and craggy – and much in between. Wandering the Oregon coast is often a heady journey of discovery in the world of geology, as just a few miles can abruptly change in scenery and landscape, with each one telling a wild geologic tale.

One of those is the more rounded rocky areas you see around Depoe Bay – and in some spots around Yachats, among others. They're less pokey versions of the more craggy, sharp edges you find in most basalts.

These are called pillow basalts. Not because they're suitable for laying your head on – indeed they're as hard as any of that black rock that typifies the Oregon coast. It's for their more rounded structure, a kind of bubble shape in a way.

Pillow basalt happens when hot lava hits the water by erupting on the ocean floor or when it flows into water from land – something which happened often around these coastal parts some 14 to 40 million years ago.

As they ooze out into the cold ocean, they quickly form in the shape of some kind of lobe and the outer surface chills immediately. But lava was at times still erupting underneath and pushing its way upwards, which then caused the newly-formed object to crack, and more lava would push out from that opening, forming yet another lobe bud.

Sometimes, these would break off and cool into giant, singular masses. Others would cool in vast formations of them – like a bed of pillow basalt structures. These had an interesting way of "settling" into the gaps between the other lobes and formations, causing accumulations of them.

These can sometimes be hundreds of meters thick.

Millions of years of lying around beneath the ocean, rising and falling in height over those eons, and being worn away by water and elements caused these to round out even further.

In the Depoe Bay area, the pillow basalts have been dated at about 14 to 17 million years ago, which means they were part of the Columbia River basalt flow way back then.

Picturing Oregon back then is a frightening scene. Periodically, probably hundreds to millions of times over millions of years, massive lava flows would erupt from what is now near eastern Oregon, traveling across 300 or so miles before it hit the ocean and mud formations just offshore. It would sizzle and destroy everything in its path.

If you want to see some astounding remnants of this, go to the main falls at Silver Falls State Park. There, a placard shows a fossilized tree that nearly burned away during this march of deadly molten rock.

This flow is called the Columbia River Basalts, mostly because they literally created the rock the Columbia River now consists of. Most striking about this magma monster is that it came from a soft spot in the Earth back then – the one that now powers Yellowstone National Park. The continental plates have moved: the soft spot stayed in the same place.

All this created not just Depoe Bay but major landmarks along the coast like Neahkahnie Mountain, Cape Meares, Yaquina Head and more. Almost all the major headlands of the northern half of the coastline were created from this: except for Cape Perpetua and Cascade Head. (See the Lincoln City book in this series for what Cascade Head really is).

Those headlands were created by a different process than Depoe Bay's basalt – but of the same lava flow. So why do they look different?

Dr. Scott Burns is a professor of geology at Portland State University. He said early geologists were stumped by all this too, but it was PSU's Martin Beeson who famously tested many of the rocks around the coastline and found they had the same geochemical signature as the basalts from the Columbia River and those known to have come from the great hole in the east.

While referred to as Grande Ronde basalts, they're technically all Columbia basalts.

The difference between Depoe Bay's pillow basalts and the more craggy shapes of Tillamook Head or Cape Foulweather is that this area was just above the water when all this fiery action was taking place.

"It has to do with being subaerial; that area of the land was above the water," Burns said. "They were flowing into shallow water – generally it was shallow water. That part of the coast at a particular time was in very shallow water. Therefore we have pillow basalts."

Back 14 to 17 million years ago, this area was somewhere about 20 miles offshore. Continental plates wouldn't drift to this position for another seven million years or so. Almost all the coast was under water, and consisting of muddy areas at the ocean floor.

Except for this patch around Depoe Bay: pillow basalts extend from about Fishing Rock State Recreation Area down to Rocky Creek State Scenic Viewpoint. This means this section was just above the water when the lava came here – or subaerial. That's about three, four miles of bubbly shapes. Basalts return to their normal structure just north of Depoe Bay at Boiler Bay, and then right about Otter Crest Loop, south of town.

Part of the action here is the fact those lavas came plunging into the ocean and into that muddy stuff offshore. This cooked that mud, Burns said, creating mudstone. He said you can see many spots on the coast where hardened mudstone is right next to basalt.

At one time there was much more of that mudstone, such as around here in the Depoe Bay area. But it was uplifted – probably a few times – and much of it eroded away. Around here, that resulted in the pillow basalts showing to the world.

You can find plenty around Depoe Bay's downtown area, but they're more common and more dramatic at the secretive north end (accessed by Sunset Ave.) and at Fishing Rock State Scenic Recreation Area, between Depoe Bay and Lincoln City.

Depoe Bay Bridge and History

You often don't pay attention to this gem as you pass over it, doing your best to balance gawking at the ocean with driving in traffic. The bridge at Depoe Bay, designed by famed architect Conde B. McCullough, is a striking construction, spanning over what is claimed to be the "world's smallest navigable harbor." It allows a scenic walk above, looking out over the always dramatic wave action of the tiny town, and it allows you to walk underneath to catch glimpses of the tiny bay and the raucous channel.

The bridge and this part of 101 were constructed in 1927 by the Kuckenberg-Wittman Company of Portland. It clocks in at 312 feet in length and the main span is a 150-foot rib deck arch. That first version was only 18 feet wide and had no sidewalks. Still, it became popular with tourists who wanted to watch boats enter the channel – as they do still. The area quickly grew in popularity after that, with the spouting horn, the aquarium and that irresistible bridge. Traffic became a problem on that tiny bridge, and the Oregon Highway Department decided to do something about it in 1939.

Oregon officials added on to the structure, making it nearly 50 feet wide, not including sidewalks, while keeping McCullogh's signature arch design. The new additions were completed in about a year, before the end of 1940.

In those early days of what was called the Roosevelt Highway, it only took four and a half hours to get from Depoe Bay to Vancouver, Washington, according to one highly publicized trip at the time.

Tourism would've really kicked into high gear after 1940 were it not for the war years, which halted all tourism development along the Oregon coast. Rubber shortages, gas rations and even strictly enforced blackouts (for fear of Japanese invaders) killed all that, and many businesses dried up. Ironically, others shifted gears and thrived as they rented out housing to military men set to keep guard over these shores.

There is an interesting document from the North Lincoln County History Museum where a general in charge of the military presence in Lincoln County severely chided much of what would later become Lincoln City for not observing the blackouts – but noting residents around Depoe Bay did. One night they set out a patrol boat from Newport to what was then called Roads End (one of the towns later to become part of Lincoln City), and found several lights on. In a newspaper op-ed, he threatened marshal law on the area.

These days, the bridge and its walkway underneath are an especially engaging way to simply kick around for awhile. At night, during stormy weather, it's a thoroughly riveting place to watch the ocean crash against the concrete of the channel, and still stay relatively dry.

Depoe Bay History: Tsunami Damage of 2011 and 1964

The big, looming threat to the entire Oregon coast is the coming mega quake offshore and the tsunami that will inevitably follow. It could happen 100 years from now; it could happen tomorrow. On average, such a subduction zone quake happens around here every 200 – 500 years. Hence all the tsunami escape route signs.

The last great mega quake in these parts was in 1700.

Scientists know that date for a number of reasons, not the least of which is documentation of a tsunami in Japan that year, all of it coinciding with native legends and consistent evidence in the soil of a massive tsunami that matches that time period.

What tsunamis and surges do on this coastline has had some dark results in modern times: most recently in 1964 and then in 2011. Both are parts of history somewhat tucked away, but very dramatic.

The nasty earthquake in Alaska in 1964 caused a significant tsunami on the Oregon coast – one which washed out chunks of Seaside, Cannon Beach and parts of the southern coast. It was even lethal near the Depoe Bay area. While the 2011 event resulted in almost nothing along this coastline except a lot of frayed nerves, Depoe Bay and some parts of the southern coast did get damaged. Something often forgotten – but it shouldn't be.

Back in March of 2011, a magnitude 9.0 undersea megathrust earthquake hit off the coast of Japan. It resulted in a tsunami of epic proportions that tore up much of the country's eastern edge, and a nuclear power plant disaster that left chunks of that surrounding area radioactive. It also created a tsunami alert here in Oregon (and with it plenty of lingering, eye-rolling conspiracy theories about "Fukushima radiation" infecting the ocean around here).

Along the Oregon coast, the tsunami warnings blared throughout the night and wee hours, causing rushes of locals to leave towns like Florence, Cannon Beach and more. By 6 a.m. or so, when nothing significant slammed into Hawaii, it became apparent the Oregon coast was safe and all tsunami alerts were lessened to watches for a surge. There is indeed footage of dimwits getting knocked over as they tried to catch snapshots of tidal surges, and one man on the south coast tried daring this tide and was swept into the ocean by just such a larger-than-usual wave.

That surge hit around 7 a.m. But not much else. So many in the Depoe Bay area, including its harbormaster and other boaters, figured the threat was over. About 11 a.m., a man named Roman Smolcic and his girlfriend boarded their charter boat "Morning Star" to prepare for a day of fun.

This was four hours after the surge lightly tapped the coastline. Harbormaster Phil Shane was hanging out on the docks, while those aboard the Morning Star worked. Suddenly, the water at the bay mouth started acting strangely, and both Shane and Smolcic are quoted in The Oregonian as seeing the wave getting "bigger and bigger."

Something was really wrong.

Smolcic decided to start filming. That may have not been the wisest move as that wave quickly began to get dangerous. Indeed, a group of people yelled at the Morning Star occupants to get out, but the massive wave was already there.

Within 30 seconds of the first surge, the dock his boat was attached to broke. There was no way he could leave. Smocic's crab pots were yanked into the bay and swirling dangerously around him as well.

You can can see his video at www.beachconnection.net/depoebay, but several other dramatic videos exist as well. All of them show the docks getting ripped apart, debris slamming into boats and pilings, and there's that very eerie sound of a kind of screeching, wailing noise, as steel and wood are being pushed around like small toys. Smolcic's video of being in the middle of it is dramatic beyond belief.

At one point, the surge appeared to be over and things calmed. Shane darted out in a small boat to rescue Smolcic and his girlfriend, and managed to barely do just that before yet another surge came in. Shane was able to jump on land just in time: that next surge grabbed his boat and batted it around.

The strange nightmare didn't end there. More surges came and went all day. It emptied out then filled back up again for hours.

Those repeated surges knocked out five docks in Depoe Bay, causing hundreds of thousands of dollars in damage in the end.

On the southern Oregon coast, Brookings and Gold Beach suffered much worse, with dozens of boats getting wrecked in their bays.

1964's quake in Alaska was a much bigger tragedy for the Oregon coast. In fact, Seaside geologist Tom Horning was a teen when that surge came roaring through Seaside, and it went right through the first floor of the building where his bedroom was, part of the family property on the Necanicum River. See the Seaside and Cannon Beach books in this series for the full story on all that. Strangely, something good did come out of that tsunami up north. Cannon Beach's Sandcastle Contest was born out of the tidal melee.

Just south of Depoe Bay, however, it proved deadly. This was March 27 – Good Friday, actually. Easter weekend.

Monte and Rita McKenzie, along with their four children and

dog, had come down to Beverly Beach (immediately south of Otter Rock and technically part of Newport) from their home in Tacoma, Washington. The family had fashioned a nifty driftwood shelter, where the parents and kids - Ricky, 6, Louie, 8, Bobby, 7, and Tammy, 3 years old - had settled in to sleep.

About 11:30 p.m., the family was awakened by a small wave that came rushing in and nearly drowned them. There was a foot of space with air inside the driftwood shelter, and the boys reportedly had trouble reaching that. Hurriedly, with some water still swirling around, they started for the pathway to their car. Except it wasn't quick enough.

A second surge came tearing in.

Rita had hold of two of the kids; Monte held on to the other two. Suddenly, she was thrown 400 yards up the beach, unable keep hold of the little ones. She was rendered unconscious by the tide, and later quoted as saying she had no idea what happened. "No one had a chance," she told a Corvallis newspaper from a hospital room that weekend.

Monte too lost hold of the kids when he was thrown up against a cliff. He as able to scramble back up the hill and get help.

The four kids and the dog were all swept out to sea. Only the body of one boy was found.

As horrific as it is, it's a tale probably not told enough; to serve as warnings for those who don't take the ocean seriously. Or in the case of the one man who was killed on the south coast in 2011, those who don't take tsunami surges seriously enough, either.

Depoe Bay – the Bay and Shell Ave.

On the southern side of the bridge you'll find the vehicle entrance to the bay. Down here, there's plenty o' parking for big rigs with boats in tow, fish-cleaning facilities, and an all around sense of calm and serenity as the waves gently plop and splash against the docks and pavement.

At night, this is especially lovely, with the lights dancing on the water and the stars gleaming overhead. That is, if the stars are showing, of course.

World's Smallest Navigable Harbor

Depoe Bay boasts the claim of "world's smallest navigable harbor," but in fact there is no official designation of any such thing. No one's keeping real records on this. But in any case, it is charming and it certainly is tiny, and there's surprisingly a lot to see.

Besides the thrill of watching vessels wandering in and out, simply checking out this body of water from the bridge viewpoints just below the roadway is a kick, especially if harbor seals are cavorting about. Sometimes fishermen are cleaning and gutting their catches at stainless steel stations above the water and tossing the unusable chunks down there, and it's immense fun to watch the seals vie for morsels.

Depoe Bay Whale and Shark Museum

A variety of deep insights into the whales, sharks and other sea critters of the coastline. Entrance fee. 234 US-101, Depoe Bay, Oregon. (541) 912-6734

Depoe Bay Visitors Center / Chamber

Gobs of information about the Depoe Bay area, including lots of regional brochures you can't get online. 223 US-101, Depoe Bay, Oregon. Www.depoebaychamber.org. (877) 485-8348.

Secret Spots: Viewpoints Behind Downtown

On the very southern edge of the bridge sit two stellar yet unknown features of Depoe Bay. Two secret diminutive viewpoints hide behind the building containing the visitor center. They can only be found by strolling around the area and the bridge, which is something you want to do anyway: the bridge is full of scenic eye-candy.

The first viewpoint is part of the lawn area found between the first two buildings on that southern edge of the bridge: the second building houses a famed restaurant and the Depoe Bay Visitors Center. You can walk down the grassy slope a bit and take in a closer look at the vessels wandering the channel, or simply get a different and really interesting new angle on the bridge and the bay. It's not a bad patch of ground to watch for whales.

On the south face of that building, about 50 feet worth of road darts westward – a strictly one-way road, which then turns into Coast Drive. At that intersection, another small viewpoint sits: simply a bench on a slight and paved outcropping. There's no way down to the rocks here. It's merely all about gazing out to sea. It's an especially calming and pleasant little viewpoint, plain and unadorned, with just the sound of the buoy's bell and the visage of waves smacking the rocks below.

It's actually a better view than the secret park down this road.

Depoe Bay's Teeny, Tiny Secret Park

While the lovely burgh's claim of "world's smallest navigable harbor" is likely not real, it is indeed possible it's got the smallest park on the whole of the Oregon coast. It's fairly new - and it's quite the secret.

Tucked away behind a bundle of bushes and trees, along a cliffside road that's much less traveled, the tiny space is full of eye-popping views. Yet it's unknown to even many locals.

It's called Depoe Bay Scenic View Park, and it's only been around since the mid 2010s. Two years after its installation did it finally acquire an official name placard and a small staircase leading up to its entrance pathway.

You'll miss it if you blink. The miniature park is hidden behind an even tinier entrance, which sits along Coast Drive, almost caddy corner from the back of the fire station (but about a block and a half down). Marked only by that small sign – which looks more like some whimsical lawn decoration at first glance – your only real clue is that small railing and three steps.

First, you enter a forested path that's short but magical, engulfing you in green foliage and a vibe that's a little reminiscent of Harry Potter. It's about a 30-foot walk, if that. Then you come to a clearing with an impressive view and a bench. And that's it. That's all there is.

The clearing itself is perhaps 20 feet long by ten feet. There's a sheer drop below, hidden by trees, and a couple of cleared spots that seem like pathways, which essentially lead you to nothing except maybe your doom if you try to venture down.

From Depoe Bay Scenic View Park, you can see just the tip of downtown, what the spouting horn is up to, and the waves crashing over the finger-like basalt of yet another glorious secret in Depoe Bay: the North Point area.

To the south, you can see part of the – again secretive - South Point section of town and its interesting combo of basalt and sandstone cliffs.

Back in 2016, Peg Leoni was owner of Trollers Lodge. She had also been a member of the planning commission in town. She said the park was actually built in 2014 when a work crew came in, hacked away the foliage and put in the bench. The signage and steps came early in 2016 and without any fanfare.

You can't actually park on Coast Drive where Depoe Bay Scenic View Park is, so it's best to park on Highway 101 by the fire station, then walk the almost two blocks south.

Hidden Access: South Point

At the extreme southern and northern tips of town you have two deliriously engaging hidden spots. Look for South Point St. at the southern end or Sunset Avenue at the north, and you'll find a set of cliffs where few others are and where all sorts of wondrous things happen that don't occur anywhere else nearby.

Both boast cliffs about 30 feet above the surf, and it's generally non-stop action here. South Point is a bit more of a delicate situation as you're wandering in front of people's homes as you meander along these awe-inspiring rockfaces. Like North Point, you're also parking in someone else's neighborhood. Be considerate as you do so.

This stretch of bubble shapes and craggy edges is much like the North Point area, but with even larger, more spectacular crevices dotting its basalt expanse. It's even more fun because it's actually not as easy to climb around on, and parts of it zigzag downward to rocky shelves close to the waves, often where glittering, colorful tidepools dwell.

You have to watch it here more, however. All that green sea goo covering these stretches is pretty slippery. You can not only slip and crack your head more easily but you can loose your footing and tumble to your watery demise.

Still, the ocean drama here is hypnotizing.

Fishing off these shelves is a favorite activity here as well.

Whale Cove and Little Whale Cove Island Reserve

Not that you can get there, or even see much of these rocks, but Whale Cove is now protected as part of the Oregon Islands National Wildlife Refuge.

This was made official in 2015, thanks to a partnership between the property owner and federal, state, and nonprofit organizations.

The Oregon Islands National Wildlife Refuge system includes 762 acres of coastal rocks, islands and headlands along 320 miles of Oregon's shoreline. These refuges provide nesting habitat for most of Oregon's 1.2 million nesting seabirds, and a large percentage of Oregon's seal and sea lion population use the various refuges to rest and produce their young.

You can see Whale Cove from a distance at Rocky Creek State Scenic Viewpoint.

The gated community there does have a private viewing area on the rocky bluffs near the islands.

Rocky Creek State Scenic Viewpoint

This one is chock of full of surprises and discoveries – and it's a lot bigger than it looks.

A sliver south of Depoe Bay, as you're winding those crazed, tight corners between Whale Cove and the southern face of Cape Foulweather, a rather magnificent view explodes out in front of you. It's the first of many, and it's called Rocky Creek State Scenic Viewpoint. If you're not careful you'll miss the turnoff, however, and thus – very literally – a front row seat to Oregon coast scenes of a multitude of moods and attitudes.

If you're looking for calming, tranquil sea vistas, this place has it, except maybe on the more powerful of stormy days. Then if you're looking for jaw-dropping wave action, this place has it as well.

Rocky Creek State Scenic Viewpoint is essentially a set of cliffs that zig-zag along this part of the central coast between Newport and Depoe Bay, with basalt bluffs that cause the waves to batter on a consistent basis. Lofty vantage points grace practically every inch of it, allowing intense viewing of every splashy moment. They're high enough that it's easy to gaze over the top of the wild breakers and take in the more distant and calm sea surface beyond them.

There are restroom facilities here that make it a nice stop along your travels, but there is also a huge array of strolling fun to be had as the cliffs meander back and forth between viewing north, directly west and then looking to the south. A lengthy, sturdy fence along the sides of the cliffs keeps you, your kids and pets from falling off the edges in most spots.

The various cracks and crevices along here can be dazzling, especially on the more violent wave height days. Rocky Creek is also known for spraying up large amounts of sea mist on a constant basis – it manages to keep you damp to fairly soaked. So watch that action with your camera and its delicate, not-so-sea-friendly mechanisms. It's not uncommon to get your gear soggy after just one or two shots and then have to clean it vigorously.

Parking is aplenty here. Numerous picnic benches lodged next to the views make for outstanding culinary moments outdoors.

A huge favorite in this park is the bench situated near one of the tips of the headland. Astounding scenes of not just heavy waves but calmer waters can be had here as well, especially if the sun is shining bright, which turns the ocean to a deep blue.

Just beyond the restroom areas – which sit about 60 feet away from the parking lot – is a somewhat untouched and slightly secretive area to Rocky Creek Scenic Viewpoint that stretches to the north. It allows access to more tidepool areas and fascinating views of Whale Cove (where some historians believe Sir Frances

Drake hung out in the summer of 1579 – and not in California as is generally accepted).

You'll find loads of engaging sights here, including rocky shelves filled with all manner of sea life as well as the destructive, deadly power of the ocean – so don't tread too far from the vegetation line viewpoints. You'll just be asking for a visit by the Grim Reaper.

Rocky Creek Scenic Viewpoint is known for its whale watching possibilities as whales do often cavort around Whale Cove, and there is some seal and sea lion viewing as well. It is part of the state park system and is sometimes referred to as Rocky Creek State Wayside.

Roaring Ledges of Rodea Point

Almost immediately after the exit from Rocky Creek State Scenic Viewpoint you'll bump into the option of heading onto Otter Crest Loop Road or continue on Highway 101. If you're lucky you'll notice the unembellished and plain gravel pullout at the beginning of the road, and if you're smart you'll stop there.

This is Rodea Point, one of the area's great pleasures. This is yet another remarkable chunk of rocky shoreline where things explode more often than not.

Not well marked, Rodea Point is basically an informal viewpoint where a gravel pullout allows the traveler more means of watching massive waves do their pyrotechnics. In a lot of ways, it is a hidden spot. Or at least it's underutilized and overlooked.

It doesn't happen all the time: but certainly more than half the time in the winter and spring months you'll find these basalt ledges battered by some enormous waves. They can tower far above you, often by 20 feet or more, then crash on these rocks with an intense, even frightening noise. Luckily, you're on the gravel area, which doesn't get hit. But those jagged, pointy chunks of rocks sloping some 30 feet downward do get smacked, and it's spectacular.

Because of this, you'll want to stay away from the temptation to go walking down to these ledge areas. This is an area that can and will kill.

Even when conditions are pretty calm other places, Rodea Point is making a spectacle. It takes a nearly glass-like ocean to still things here; that is actually rare.

At night, especially if the moon is lighting up things at all, things really get crazy and mesmerizing. Those sounds are seemingly even louder and more startling, though maybe that's just the lack of traffic noise after hours. It's highly suggested you spend at least a few minutes listening to as well as watching that ocean after dark. You'll likely find yourself staying much longer.

Hiking the Oregon Coast Trail South of Depoe Bay

As mentioned in the previous listing about the Oregon Coast Trail at Boiler Bay, the trail runs along the highway and then down the sidewalks of Depoe Bay. At its southern end, hiking means walking the dangerous highway again a couple of miles until you reach Otter Crest Loop Road. There, a bike lane allows you a little more safety than the raging highway: at least cars are forced to move slowly here.

Then, you reach Cape Foulweather. From there, it's about a mile on the small roadway (now it's a two-lane stretch rather than one-way), until you reach Otter Rock and the Devil's Punchbowl. From there, descend the long stairway to Otter Rock's northern face, and you've got about four miles of beach to walk until 62nd St. at Newport.

Otter Crest Loop

It all begins just south of Rocky Creek State Scenic Viewpoint, as 101 twists around tight corners between Depoe Bay and Newport. The highway rises suddenly as you head south, but off to the right there's a mysterious little road junction. This is Otter Crest Loop, which meanders beneath 101 for a while, until it ends up high atop Cape Foulweather, winds past Otter Rock and the Devil's Punchbowl and then meets up again with 101 a ways north of Newport.

This lulling but lively stretch of roadway is one of the more stunning along the Oregon coast, and yet it's fairly forgotten. You can't get the full effect coming from Newport, from the south: most of this road is one-way heading towards the south. You have to start at the northern edge, where you get a preview of the coming wonders at the pullout called Rodea Point. There, the breakers go bonkers on even fairly calm days.

The northern edge of Otter Crest Loop provides a nice assemblage of secretive wonders hiding in plain sight – along a tiny route which in itself is quite clandestine. Among them a cajoling but not-very-well-known lookout spot next to a scenic bridge, and then there's some stunning trails literally hiding off to the side of the road. A little less than a mile from Rodea Point the road becomes a one-way, where a handful of official and unofficial pullouts beckon, and you get glimpses of dramatic, plunging cliffs and the unobtainable, violent beaches below them.

After a mile or so, you end up at the parking lot of Cape Foulweather and its astounding vistas.

Ben Jones Bridge – Rocky Creek and Ben Jones Bridge Viewpoint

A mere 100 feet after Rodea Point you'll bump into the Rocky Creek Bridge – also known as the Ben Jones Bridge. It was built in 1927 and stands at MP 130.03. There's a mini-turnout here to watch the surf go bonkers – and it does.

There are no facilities here, but there's a rounded stone wall that boasts plenty of atmosphere and parking for a handful of cars. It's tiny but it's wondrous.

It's all above a mini-cove of sorts, where oceanic drama is the norm. Even in calmer weather, these rocky bluffs provide a fair amount of action. When the stormier waves hit – wow. Those cliffs are 50 feet or so above the ocean, and it's not abnormal to see them launch practically above the grassy topsoil.

The cove seems to shelter the lookout from such batterings, however.

Otter Crest Loop Begins – Wacky History

Otter Crest Loop is a curiosity among coastal drives. It was actually part of the original Highway 101 back in the '20s. But by the '30s, the newer stretch (above the loop, the route we all drive today) was built, rendering the loop obsolete. It was actually closed off for a year or two, considered a useless extra. Local residents, however, protested, wanting to keep the scenic drive, and after only a year or so the loop was opened again.

For a long time, Otter Crest Loop was a two-way.

The whole reason this is a one-way is because of numerous landslides coming down that high slope. That is, after all, primarily soil between here and 101 above. There was a handful of them over the decades, with a couple of especially heavy ones in the '90s that actually closed the road.

Sometimes it came from above; sometimes it was the westward edge of the road itself. That seaward side started to shrink.

Then came one big, gnarly slide in the mid '90s. A whole chunk of the southbound lane left the cliff behind. Caught in that landslide was a man and his son in their van: the vehicle slid down the muddy sludge with them inside. The passengers were able to crawl back up the cliff and were rescued.

After that, for many years this stretch was a foot-path only, blocked off by a concrete barrier. Work was delayed on it for a long time and then proceeded slowly once it did. This was a surreal chapter in the Otter Crest Loop Road history. It didn't take long for nature to start reclaiming this segment. By the late '90s, this hiking-only road became more and more covered by fir needles and drifting soil. The roadway started to disappear and it began to look like a scene from that TV show "Life After People." Chunks of the road just dipped off into oceanic oblivion. It was eerie but exceptionally beautiful.

I walked it a few times myself in this state and found it truly unforgettable.

Finally, it was reopened in the early 2000's as a one-way road with a bike lane. They had done considerable work with all kinds of shoring up and concrete structures tucked away beneath the road, some of which were obviously built to drain runoff from the rains.

Secret Spot: Cliffs Below Otter Crest Loop Road

You could nickname them the Clandestine Cliffs of Lincoln County. They're a set of basalt ledges that form some of the most spectacular finds along this shoreline – and they're a full-on secret. This is probably a good thing, since there are no barriers to keep you from falling off these black beauties, which tower around 40 feet or more above the ocean. In fact, in 2018 someone did meet their maker in this spot. Don't ever take kids down here – and stay well back from the edges.

How to find it?

For almost a mile past Rodea Point, the road is still two lanes. Past the Ben Jones Bridge lookout, and past a brief cluster of neighborhood homes, there's a sudden curve and the road abruptly turns into one lane. At this bend, there's a gravel pullout: this is the entrance to the secret trails.

There's no break in the guard rail. No sign indicating anything. You simply have to stop at the pullout and look over the guard rail for the beginning of a pathway. It's a steep one in spots, and absolutely not advisable in muddy conditions.

This hidden trail zigzags its way through tall brush, sometimes with prickly plants, then into a patch of dark, primeval forest. It's at once magical, mystical and slightly spooky. Finding freaky-shaped mushrooms along the way is not uncommon, and they're often large and in wild, dazzling colors. The trail meanders into the grass and through poison oak leafs (so be careful and keep to long pants).

Then, suddenly, you walk out of the forest and the ocean expanse literally explodes in front of you. It's abrupt and truly dramatic. Your jaw will drop: guaranteed. These cliffs are rugged, untouched and completely primitive and pristine. It feels like it's out of Narnia or Middle Earth or something. There's little, maybe even nothing, like it on the coast.

You'll quickly find these fascinating basalt structures have sometimes left flat, seat-like structures for you to sit and watch the waves smack this wonder zone – a literal front row seat to the drama, thanks to nature.

Another cliff lies not far away from this initial one, more difficult to get to because of the thick brush, but even more clandestine and more full of surprises. A path worn into the grass will get you there.

Whales sometimes lazily saunter past, and you can hear them blowing their spouts and see them doing other awe-inspiring things.

Viewpoints Along the One-Way

You don't have to hit the big secret trail to get an unforgettable eyeful.

So many more such views are available from Otter Crest Loop before you get to Cape Foulweather, albeit from the roadway (and less of a strenuous jaunt). Plunging cliffs disappear into raging surf. Dramatic ocean vistas pop out between the thick walls of soothing forest. Dazzling oceanic pyrotechnics are in abundance. Grassy greens cover the blackened basalt towers. Plus, you can see Cape Foulweather and the little gift shop atop it from new angles.

Every 200 to 300 feet there's some new, amazing sight to check out. Some pullouts are obvious; others look somewhat sketchy because they're so small you may be sticking your car out into traffic to some degree.

There's only one rule: have your camera ready. OK, two rules: watch for bike and hiker traffic and be cautious when pulling over constantly to take in the views and vistas. Because you will indeed pull over constantly.

Cape Foulweather

A mere few miles south of Depoe Bay, two major landmarks have sparked the imaginations of generations – one for at least hundreds of years. Cape Foulweather is a basalt headland that is large enough to change weather systems on either side of it, while the Devil's Punchbowl is an intriguing cave where the tide swirls spectacularly and angrily. You can get an aerial view of the Punchbowl from this lofty point.

About four miles south of Depoe Bay, and roughly that many miles north of Newport, Cape Foulweather looms like a giant watchful being. It stands about 500 feet above the sea, and is accessed by a somewhat winding tangle of roads that connect from a very twisting section of 101. Here, a small parking lot and viewpoint allow visitors panoramic vistas, including this magnificent nearly-aerial view of Otter Rock, its odd beaches and the famed Devil's Punchbowl below. Hit it all at the right time and you'll find the Punchbowl painted by the warm rays of the waning sunset. Other times, giant fingers of fog interlace with it in a striking manner.

Fog – or least low-lying clouds – occasionally performs this miraculous stunt where it's flying upwards and above the cape, like a rushing stream of wispy ghosts. The clouds get rammed up against one side of the cliffs, so you see this fast-moving mist come up from below, then it's sent skyrocketing in an ascent that's usually high speed. Simply dazzling.

For a serious and surreal treat, check out the area at night. If the moon is out, it often stretches its gigantic reflection across the ocean, made even more impressive by this high angle. Or perhaps the stars are out and especially bright, if the night is clear. The Milky Way looms in dizzying glory.

During sunny days this place is at its best, of course. Waters turn a vibrant blue, and whale watching is particularly easy. If you're in search of the green flash at sunset, this is a good parcel to make it to: higher vantage points can make it easier to catch that.

The other major feature is, of course, the gift shop, which has been there for decades. The old coastal stalwart once featured those coin-operated telescope thing-a-ma-bobs, but that seems to have disappeared.

Cape Foulweather was actually named by Britain's Captain James Cook in 1778, as he made his way up the coastline. Apparently he ran into some disagreeable weather, although he was somewhat impressed with the headland – enough to name it, anyway.

At the time, explorers referred to this area as New Albion.

Weird Science: Cape Foulweather Geology

There seems to be a long-standing rumor that Cape Foulweather is a volcano.

"No it's not," said Burns. In fact, he laughed when recalling those were his sentiments when he saw that the gift shop at Cape Foulweather had a sign proclaiming: "You are standing on an old volcano."

This was the thought for many decades among geologists, but radiometric dating proved it too came from those Columbia lava flows of 14 to 17 million years ago. Part of the misconception is the shape of Cape Foulweather.

"Cape Foulweather from the air looks like an old volcano," Burns said. "It's just been eroded away over thousands and thousands of years, with a big landslide in the middle that looks like a crater."

The cape's origin is a surprising one, and something that's hard for many to wrap their heads around. But it shares its origin story with that of most of the headlands like Cape Lookout,

Tillamook Head, etc.

It's actually a canyon that was once filled up with lava. Crazy, right? They're called intracanyon formations in real life (well, real life for geologists, anyway).

At one point during proto-Oregon's existence, a gigantic canyon sat here. Numerous flows came over from eastern Oregon during that Columbia basalt period, and filled it up over time. Since basalt – cooled lava – is much hardier than other rock or soil, it didn't erode. But over time, the stuff that once formed the canyon did fall away, leaving this higher object.

There was a time Yaquina Head was thought to be a volcano as well – but that was eventually disproven. More on that in the Newport book in this series later in 2019.

Over many more millions of years, even Cape Foulweather was beaten down into its current, glorious shape.

It's worth noting Pacific City's Cape Kiwanda is all sandstone, a very different structure than the basalt behemoths.

Otter Rock – Town and Rock Structure

A ways down the road from Cape Foulweather – either via Otter Crest Loop or Highway 101 – the tiny burgh of Otter Rock sits tucked away atop this narrow promontory that includes the famed Devil's Punchbowl. It's an unincorporated community of a few hundred folks, if that, featuring a seafood joint, a rather famous winery operation and one or two seasonal shops, depending on the year or time of year.

History: Naming Otter Rock, Devil's Punchbowl

According to local legends and documents provided by the Lincoln County Historical Society in Newport, Otter Rock was a place apparently called The Rock by Siletz tribes who lived here.

However, this comes from descendants of white settlers, so like the Elephant Rock tale in a coming chapter, grains of salt are in order.

Meanwhile, according to one geologic document anyway, the Devil's Punchbowl was called Satan's Cauldron around the '40s.

Numerous legends seem to swirl about regarding the names of these places, but one thing is certain: the little village and the structure seemed to share various monikers. They were loosely interchangeable, too: the village was sometimes referred to simply as "The Punchbowl," among other names.

"The Rock" - according to legend – came about because of a set of arches and pointy structures that existed at one time. Apparently well before settlers arrived, some of those landmarks had disappeared. Others disintegrated in the '30s.

In the 1800s, this area was part of a massive reservation allocated to the Siletz by the U.S. government. That was whittled down to nothing, like all reservations, and eventually 150 acres were sold to two natives, including Dope Spencer. His name resulted in two creeks along the village: Spencer Creek and Dope Creek. That was in 1894 – Spencer died only four years later.

In those early days of the settlement, even before Spencer's acquisition, the area was known for lots of otter. Purportedly, one settler did come up with that name at some point because sea otter were floating around offshore in abundance. However, a local man named Joe Biggs claimed to have shot the last one in 1906. He apparently snagged a hefty $900 for the pelt, and supposedly this is when and where the name was born.

The sea stack almost a mile west of Beverly Beach – the long, flat one way out there – is called Otter Rock as well. The rock immediately west of the Punchbowl is called Gull Rock (above).

Devil's Punchbowl, the Punch Bowl and Otter Rock became mixed up together for a few decades, even by locals. The Yaquina Bay News, dated January 21, 1922, talked about upcoming changes:

"The owners of the property are now placing it upon the market. Newport, Agate Beach and Otter Rock will soon be one resort, extending nine miles north along the ocean front to Cape Foulweather."

It notes Otter Rock was known as the "Punch Bowl" to many at the time.

In a geology paper by Parke Snavely in the '70s, he says the Punchbowl was called "Satan's Cauldron" in the '40s. No documentation on this could be found, although Snavely indicates this was a marketing name given by the then-Oregon

Highway Commission (now ODOT). So it could've been an ad slogan or nickname of some kind.

That Otter Rock land was sold to Willard Jones in 1904 for – get this - $1000. Three years after that, it was sold to the now-famous Ben Jones for $5,000.

Jones, known as the "father of Highway 101," was a key figure in the layout of Otter Rock. More on him in the next chapter. He lived there for more than 20 years, becoming a mayor of Newport and Toledo, while also being known as the unofficial mayor of the fledgling village of Otter Rock.

In the early 1900s the little town became a big hit, though most of its tourism came from Newport and Toledo. That's because travel took a half day from there to Otter Rock – a trip that is now 8 minutes max in bad traffic. From Toledo the journey was a full day. It was all on foot back then, save for a lucky few that had horses. Some hopped a lumber train that ran from Toledo to Beverly Beach, then walked the remaining mile or so.

The 1920s saw a boom in tourism, but even slightly earlier than that there was the Horning Hotel, which had become a destination spot because of their cooking and legendary pies. The Horning Hotel had been built from lumber from the shipwreck of the Minnie Kelton, which crashed against Cape Foulweather, causing the death of four of her 19-man crew.

The Hornings sold the property in 1927 and it burned down shortly after – quite possibly because of a still that was brewing liquor upstairs. This was prohibition times, after all.

Like the rest of the Oregon coast, tourism fell then rose again after the stock market crash, and by the late '30s it was starting to reach a fevered pitch again until World War II happened. The entire coastline was under blackout conditions at night for a few years.

By the '80s and '90s, tourism was booming even more and many of the landmark buildings and businesses of Otter Rock got their start in there.

History: Ben Jones, "Father of Highway 101"

Jones was quite the jack of all trades, but he was known for playing a key role in the beginnings of Highway 101. Starting out as a mail carrier in the 1800s, he hated the lack of good roads between the central coast and Corvallis – his route. Essentially, this started his lifelong interest in roads in the area.

At one point he was a steamboat captain, and at another he was a lawyer, a two-time mayor and a state legislator. Jones was also instrumental in extricating Newport and other parts of Lincoln County from Benton County, because he didn't like the way coastal residents were treated by those to the east.

Eventually, he drafted legislation pushing the creation of a highway along the entire Oregon coast. In 1919, Oregon voters approved that project, partially out of recognition that the strains of World War I called for protection of the west coast, and thus better roads were needed. What was then called the Roosevelt Military Highway was born, starting work in 1921 and finishing up about ten years later.

Sadly, Jones died before the highway was finished, never getting to fully see his own work.

At Otter Rock, Jones also built a home out of lumber from the Minnie Kelton schooner. Two streets are named for his daughters: Nellie and Gladys. Another is named for his wife Ellie.

Landmark: Devil's Punchbowl, Devil's Punchbowl State Scenic Natural Area

Famous and freaky: this purveyor of tidal madness has probably been this way for hundreds if not thousands of years. A giant sea cave that once caved in, its top is now open and the swirling oceanic display visible to all.

It is a bit of a misnomer, however. The Devil's Punchbowl is not a fiery show a lot of the time, really. It's chaotic and violent if you were somehow able to get down there, of course. But only in larger storms does it really live up to the title. Most of the time, it lazily swirls about down there.

Of course, this causes more than one online reviewer to moan with disappointed self-entitlement on a regular basis. Sorry kids, the ocean isn't there for your amusement. Relax and enjoy the ruggedness and simplicity of it all.

A myriad of other shapes and wild textures fill the vista here as well.

This mini-headland and state park includes the marine gardens immediately to the north (the entrance is at the northern parking lot), and some stunning viewpoints to the south. From here you can see Newport, and in the distance the flashing of the Yaquina Head Lighthouse. There are some picnic tables and restroom facilities as well.

The northern face you can't really access: it's all occupied by homes or the giant hotel complex.

Some truly fun and funky secrets abound, including its history, a rock feature that was once iconic and more. Keep reading.

Inside Devil's Punchbowl

Normally, this wacky-colored sea cave is filled with carousing ocean waves that would be vicious and unsurvivable for humans. Sometimes it's an angry tide you get to see from above, but even in the calmer waters of summer, it's interesting to watch stuff roll around in there. You just can't imagine being there, however.

Periodically, perhaps no more than once or twice a year, extreme low tide events allow access from the beach below Otter Rock, and you can actually walk inside this raucous little cavern.

This is not something you're technically allowed to do, however. Even if this area is opened up, it's only briefly. It is very much not advisable. Oregon State Park's official position is you should not be doing that.

So for all those who will never get to see it (and again you should not), I leave this description of its insides.

All around you are weird walls of smeared and melded colors, evidence of the constant churning that goes on in there and the array of chemical processes that oxidize and paint everything. The floor is covered with all manner of marine debris, but mostly it's layered with polished stones ranging in size from large rocks to sizable boulders. It's not easy to walk about inside.

These are rare events, and you have to watch very carefully for the incoming tide, as it is swift and merciless. This isn't a place you want to get caught inside, as the canal-like rocks on the outside that sort of guard the Punchbowl's interior are often flooded with fairly high water even in these low tide events.

Really, entering and leaving the cave is the most dangerous part, and that is where I've gotten in trouble more than once. If you wait just a little too long, that tide starts coming back into the marine gardens area. Suddenly, you find yourself wading hip-deep in rather frightening water.

Summer sand levels here create a faux low tide event, sometimes for extended periods. These can allow you to get a little closer to the outer edges of the Punchbowl. Around here, weird little caves and shapes abound. One looks like part of a giant hoof. Another crack in the rocks shows light on the other side: a tiny sea cave filled with intriguing stuff when you point a flashlight down there.

Marine Gardens Near Depoe Bay

While Devil's Punchbowl gets a lot of the attention, there's a stunning, rather unpopulated beach lying just below the cliffs that never ceases to cause wonder.

The swirling, tidal madness of the Punchbowl itself is a stark contrast to the cozy little beach just below – except of course during stormy conditions, when you definitely can't even venture down there. Unless, of course, you want to see the place from the vantage point of below the waves as you take your last breath.

During lower tide events is when the marine gardens appear. It's a tidepool hunter's paradise, with numerous critters existing here.

It's all accessed via a sloped walkway between the beach and the parking lot, and then the steps to the beach are sometimes non-existent or barely intact, as winter storms tend to ravage the boundaries of this beach and take out the conveniences of Man. So there are times you'll have to crawl down the final two or three feet of the concrete walkway. Some years it takes awhile to be repaired.

Once on the beach, you'll discover a host of oddities and intricate rock structures. Like the monolithic slab of sandstone that looks like a giant boot at the tideline. Or flat rocky spots that look as if Mother Nature is asking you to "please come in and have a seat."

A mix of sandy flat areas and rocky labyrinths typify this varied place, leaving something to do for almost everyone.

It's also a big attraction for surfers at times, although they tend to hit the other side of the headland that creates Otter Rock, walking down an enormous stairway to hit the flat, sandy beach facing Newport to the south.

Be cautious here: lots of slippery green stuff covers the rocky surfaces.

When the tide gets pushed back to an extreme distance, the stretch north of this little cell gets opened up. Well, sort of. There's so much slippery algae and sea lettuce it can be worse than walking on ice. Normally, the northern point next to the marine gardens is cordoned off by the tides (though guests at the

Inn at Otter Crest have a private access).

If it is at all accessible, you may get to experience the weird little cave at that section. It spawned a wacky legend and the area was thereafter called "Little Man's Cove."

Odd History: Little Men of the Punchbowl

One of the more curious and hilarious historical tales of the Oregon coast was created at the "Punch Bowl," as it was known to many. It was Dope Spencer (mentioned previously) who had a mysterious encounter with "little flying men" near that cave. He ventured into the cove-like area just after dark and claims to have been attacked by a bunch of what he called "little flying men," filling him with terror and causing him to sprint for his life. After that, Spencer and family members never went near that area again after dark.

An article from the Statesman Journal (from around the '80s or so) documents the local residents talking about their heritage and Spencer's run-in with the tiny paranormal. Villagers thoroughly believed Spencer at the time, but the more modern interpretation is that they were clearly bats from that cave below the hotel.

Odd History: Elephant Rock at the Punchbowl, Legends

While the Devil's Punchbowl has been a heavy favorite among visitors for generations, there was actually another rock structure nearby that had the attention of tourists for quite a while before it. (Above: Elephant Rock is the structure in the foreground).

Then, in an eerie twist, a purported curse seemed to come true upon the destruction of this landmark, which now sits at a beach that's not really accessible anymore.

Right below the tiny community of Otter Rock, just north of

Newport, there was a rock structure named Elephant Rock, which looked significantly similar to an elephant with its trunk dipped into the water. According to a 1936 local newspaper article, Elephant Rock was quite a draw to tourists, who snapped many a picture of the charming formation.

In the final days of 1929, Elephant Rock was beheaded by a winter storm, altered forever as so many favorite coastal landmarks have been in these decades since Europeans began settling here. The story appeared in the local Yaquina Bay newspaper on January 2, with the headline "Elephant Rock Gone – Interesting Landmark Crumbles Away."

The article describes it as being a favorite of thousands. It was a big deal for small town news then: "While taking an automobile drive with her husband Friday, Mrs. J. J. Tobin discovered that the head and trunk of the "elephant" had fallen off and crumbled."

Later, a 1936 piece talks about the headland's only resident looking sadly upon the rocky remnant of a departed old friend.

Just then a curse fell on the area – but more on that in a bit.

According to Jodi Weeber with the Lincoln County Historical Society in Newport (back in 2011), there's supposedly a native tribe legend that goes with the rock, saying there was once a massive fire in the area that destroyed a lot of land. This was the "Fire Demon," as it was known, and the "Great Spirit" of the local people went to battle with it.

Somehow, the last of the woolly mammoths – so the legend goes – joined the fray, and beat the fire demon at the base of Otter Crest (it undoubtedly was not named that by local tribes) by dipping its trunk into the water and hosing down the flames.

From then on, the Great Spirit decided that this noble elephant, or woolly mammoth – or whatever – would stand guard against the fire demon. He was placed there in stone.

The legend says something to the effect that the local people and their forests – from Yachats to the Siletz River by Lincoln City – would be protected as long as Elephant Rock stood and as long as they kept tradition.

In a cruel, almost paranormal twist, bad luck hit the tribes big time once Elephant Rock crumbled. The article notes that the reservations for the Siletz and Grand Ronde Indians were dissolved right around this time.

Shortly after Elephant Rock's head was lost, there were major fires all around the coast, Weeber said.

"One burnt down the hill to Depoe Bay, another big one burned between Waldport and Yachats, and there was the big one in Bandon that year," Weeber said. "Two years later, there was the fire in Tillamook."

This all, of course, begs the question: how did local tribes know about Woolly Mammoths way back?

Weeber said she didn't know and laughed.

"Sounds like a white man thing to me," Weeber said. "There were a lot of stories written by the white man who say they were an Indian tale, like Jump-Off Joe at Newport."

Indeed, checking with a Siletz tribal historian, he knew of no such legend. It's something whitey made up.

That rock structure called Elephant Rock – or what's left of it – still sits on this beach, but sadly it's only accessible by those staying at the Inn at Otter Crest facility, as they've created the stairway, which is the only access to this beach. It's one of the few beaches in Oregon which has wound up not public by circumstance of the only access being private. Even at extremely low tides, you generally can't get around that second point to the north, as too many slippery algaes dominate the rocks there.

Origin of Devil's Punchbowl: Trippy Geology

Whatever it was called or simply nicknamed, we now know it as the Devil's Punchbowl, the swirling pot of oceanic, boiling madness that gets especially frothy during storms.

Did you ever wonder how the Punchbowl came to be? How it was formed? And what sort of odd secrets are embedded in its ancient walls?

Essentially it's an old, old – very old – sea cave that fell apart. But there's more to the story.

A large paper on the subject was written in the '70s by Parke D. Snavely, Jr. and Norman S. Macleod for Oregon's geology division, called "Visitor's Guide to the Geology of the Coastal Area Near Beverly Beach State Park, Oregon."

According to these geology documents from the State of Oregon in 1971, the Devil's Punchbowl is made of bedded sandstone and siltstone of the Astoria Formation. The material that comprises it is maybe as old as 18 million years, having been a kind of fill-in of a variety of sandstone materials and other rocks, coming from eroded basalt from around Oregon, the Gorge and other sources.

Sandstone is much more easily eroded than sturdy basalt, and depending on what else it's mixed with, can be eaten away quite quickly in geologic terms. For instance, the structure known as Jump-Off Joe in Newport is made up of sandstone and has been fading rather fast since it emerged as a headland, perhaps a little over one hundred years ago. Cape Kiwanda at Pacific City too is crumbling fairly quickly in spots

The Devil's Punchbowl was carved into a sea cave sometime in its distant past, and then somewhere after that the holes in the rock structure just got bigger and bigger as the tide ate at it. Eventually, the top of the sea cave fell in, creating that huge bowl-like structure you now see.

At some point over the millennia this sandstone existed, rock-boring clams made their homes in these channels going into the Punchbowl. Such holes are still visible today during extreme low tide events. Also, wood fossils have been found in the structure of the Punchbowl as well.

Snavely and Macleod say in their paper that beneath the Punchbowl is a weaker-than-usual bedrock, which is called a volcanic breccia because it's a mixture of basalt and other stuff.

"This breccia formed when hot lava was explosively injected into wet sediments," the scientists said. "This explosive action probably shattered the overlying rocks and produced an easily eroded circular area."

An interesting side note: the Astoria Formation shows up as landmarks like Jump-Off Joe and many of the sea cliffs from Nye Beach, through Moolack Beach and Beverly Beach, up to the Devil's Punchbowl. It's yellow and gray, and sometimes a dark gray, depending on what's mixed in.

Larger fossils have been found in these layers, including a kind of prehistoric hippopotamus and ancient sea lions. Some of these fossils were collected as far north as Gleneden Beach and have been on display at the Smithsonian.

The best view of this formation is the dark gray, rutted and groove-filled bedrock that shows up at Moolack Beach during really low sand levels in winter. All kinds of fossils are found in there: it's astounding.

Odd Find: Secret Ghost Forest Stump

As mentioned in the previous chapter on ghost forests, a rather secret one resides near the bottom of the staircase below Otter Rock. Watch the tides: this isn't always accessible. The other one, of course, sits at the entrance to Beverly Beach.

Local History: Pathfinders and Primitive Roads

In 1912, a small group of intrepid explorers did something strenuous and maybe a little insane at the time: they drove their automobiles that crazy 24-mile stretch along the central Oregon coast, between Newport and Lincoln City.

That's right. This was a completely nutty venture at this point.

Sure, it's something we all take for granted these days, taking maybe a half hour to 45 minutes, depending on traffic. But back in 1912, when most of the roads were the beaches themselves or just extremely muddy tracks along the hills, this journey took 23 hours round trip.

That's nothing compared to the all-day drudgery it was from just Newport to Otter Rock if you were on foot.

This trek, made by the four men called Pathfinders in 1912, was re-enacted in July of 2012 as part of a special historic celebration, organized by the Lincoln County Historical Society. Organizers put out a call for vintage cars to take part in this now-much-more-comfortable journey. The car caravan from Newport to Lincoln City celebrated the 100th anniversary of the Pathfinders – the first of its kind at the time.

Back then, the goal was to promote the need for better roads to increase business and tourism as part of the Commercial Club's good roads program. The Commercial Club was a forerunner of the Chamber of Commerce. The men drove through mud, sand and surf to get there, getting stuck numerous times along the way. One famous photo shows them getting dug out of the sand at what would later be called Fogarty Beach.

To find more on Depoe Bay (including lodging) see
www.beachconnection.net/depoebay

ABOUT ANDRE' GW HAGESTEDT

Andre' Hagestedt is a writer, photographer, web designer and now, by default, a videographer, living in Portland, Oregon. He is publisher, editor and official web geek and marketer for Oregon Coast Beach Connection – beachconnection.net – a curious hybrid of online magazine and news publication covering travel, entertainment and science about the upper half of the Oregon coast.

Hagestedt was born in Freiburg Im Breisgau, in 1962, in what was then known as West Germany. For a brief time as a toddler, his father, mother and newborn brother lived on the south coast, but moved to the Salem / Keizer area shortly after. He grew up there, studying classical and jazz music until his early 20s, dabbling in writing on and off and eventually chasing a career in music and then photography.

By his 30s in the 1990s, his longtime hopes of becoming a rock musician failed, he began writing about rock music. Highlights included interviews with some of his heroes including Jethro Tull, members of King Crimson and Love and Rockets. He soon began branching out into other kinds of journalism, writing (or working for) a wide variety of publications, including Salem's Statesman Journal, The Oregonian, KXL radio in Portland, The Rocket, Eugene Weekly and more.

In the late '90s, Hagestedt set about documenting every single beach access on the northern half of the Oregon coast, which resulted in becoming editor of a short-lived tourism newspaper there, and eventually starting Oregon Coast Beach Connection in 2007.

Currently, Oregon Coast Beach Connection has a readership of almost two million per year and gets about six million pageviews per year.

Made in the USA
Las Vegas, NV
11 May 2021